Chambers

Punctuation Guide

Gordon Jarvie

EDINBURGH   NEW YORK

Published 1992 by W & R Chambers Ltd,
43-45 Annandale Street, Edinburgh EH7 4AZ

© Gordon Jarvie 1992

British Library Catalogue in Publication Data
A catalogue record for this book is available from the
British Library

ISBN 0-550-18044-3

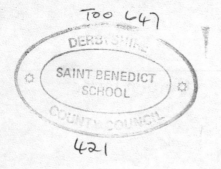
Typeset by Chatsworth Studios Ltd., Killingworth,
Newcastle upon Tyne
Printed in England by Clays Ltd., St Ives plc

Contents

Introduction

Punctuation is essential to good writing. Without it, we are hard-pressed to say where a sentence ends or a paragraph begins, or how the nuances of a text are to be understood. Yet over the last thirty years, there has been a trend in British education away from formal teaching of this basic subject, with the predictable result that generations of students – and now, alas, of teachers too – are unsure of their ground. This book has three ambitions: firstly to offer simple guidelines for writers of text; secondly to show that punctuation is easy; and thirdly to suggest that it is important. It does not pretend to be the authoritative work on the subject: that would take a much longer book. But it does try to cover all the basic aspects of punctuation. It not only covers those areas where agreement is general, but also comments on matters of stylistic preference.

Generally speaking, the times we live in favour a minimalist approach to punctuation. When we read material written in the 1950s or earlier, we are often struck by the amount of punctuation in use – excessive to our latter-day eye. This book goes along with the minimalist or utilitarian philosophy: it seldom recommends the intervention of punctuation if none is strictly necessary. However, as I have said, it also takes the view that punctuation is important, so it takes issue strongly with those time and motion experts who advise the Civil Service and other hapless bodies that secretaries can pound out more letters per hour if they do away with commas. This may be true, but it is worthless advice, and if it is followed it may well account for not a little bureaucratic gobbledygook.

There are few absolutes in good punctuation. Like so

many other aspects of language, it is a moving target. We have only to look at the King James Bible to see how very far punctuation has evolved over the last four hundred years. The advent of the typewriter, of the popular press, and most recently of the word processor, have all had a significant impact on our approach to punctuation – not always for the better.

Where possible, and appropriate, in this book – for example, with the dash – I have tried to show examples of good practice, rather than a list of 'Thou shalt not's'. Because, while I firmly believe that punctuation can – indeed must – be taught, I am also aware that one of the best ways to teach is by good example.

An asterisk has been used in front of a sentence or word, as on page 18, to signify an erroneous construction – to be avoided. But note that not every erroneous construction in the book is preceded by an asterisk; in some cases, the text is sufficiently explanatory.

I believe readers will welcome the opportunity to check their own punctuation skills. At the end of most chapters, there is a 'Check-up' section containing sentences and longer texts which need punctuating. Readers are invited to complete these exercises, and check their accuracy against the answers offered at the end of the book.

1

The Full Stop

1.1 A preliminary note on the sentence

It makes little sense to talk about punctuation marks without a word on the sentence. The *Oxford English Dictionary* calls a sentence 'such a portion of composition or utterance as extends from one full stop to another'. *Chambers English Dictionary* calls it 'a number of words making a complete grammatical structure, in writing generally begun with a capital letter and ended with a full stop or its equivalent'. For the purposes of this book, let us define a sentence as a group of words that makes sense, that contains a verb, that begins with a capital letter and ends with a full stop or its equivalent (a question mark or exclamation mark).

1.2 The full stop as the end of a sentence

The full stop or period is the basic punctuation point. Everyone knows that it indicates the end of a sentence. If you take the view that sentences should be short and simple, you will be happy to see a text with lots of full stops in it. Because usually that means a text that is easy to read.

In formal or correct English, a sentence is usually an indication by the writer of a complete, unified thought. In most simple sentences, a full stop is the only punctuation required:

He lives in Jamaica.
Monday was a glorious day.
Their work was hopeless.
I was completely fed up with her.
Our beach is badly polluted.

Even in some longer and more complicated sentences, a full

stop is the only punctuation required:

> I was late home on Monday because I couldn't start the car.
> She works in the evenings in order to save some money for her holidays.
> He was a keen sportsman and had won a number of trophies.
> She packed an overnight bag and left by the 10 o'clock train.

These longer sentences do not need to be broken up by a comma. Why? Because of *continuity of subject*. But the following sentences are different, and a comma is called for:

> I was late home on Monday, and my daughter had gone back to London.
> She works in the evenings, so her husband stays at home to put the children to bed.

Can you see the difference? It will be discussed further in Chapter 3 (page 12).

A common error is to use a full stop where no punctuation is necessary, or where another punctuation point should have been used:

> * He stood there. Looking at us.
> * They are at the pub. Celebrating his promotion.
> * Two people came to see us. One called Andy and one called Sally.

What should we write?

> He stood there looking at us.
> They are at the pub celebrating his promotion.
> Two people came to see us – one called Andy and one called Sally.
> *or*
> Two people came to see us. One was called Andy and one was called Sally.

For purposes of emphasis, it is possible to use a full stop in the following context, even though it does not conclude a sentence:

I do not disagree with you. On the contrary.
He was not distressed by the criticism. Far from it.
I object. Comprehensively.
I love you. Honestly. Believe me.

There is a sort of compression (called ellipsis) at work here. *On the contrary*, *Far from it*, *Comprehensively* and *Honestly* are not real sentences. The implication of these statements gives the following complete sentences:

I do not disagree with you. On the contrary, I agree with you.
He was not distressed by the criticism. Far from it – he throve on it.
I object, and I object comprehensively.
I love you. Honestly I do. Believe me when I say this.

Stylistically, the earlier versions are better because much more succinct.

Unpunctuated text gives the stilted robot-effect of 'computer-speak'. Readers cannot begin to guess the tone required, indeed they may find it difficult to establish the basic meaning. They soon run out of breath if trying to read unpunctuated text aloud. Try it with the following text, and then see if you can put in the full stops.

Cinderella entered the room on her hands diamond rings glittered on her head a rich tiara sparkled among the golden curls on her pretty little feet two glass slippers gleamed as she swirled through the room in a beautiful silken gown Prince Charming strode towards her (five full stops)

If you get the full stops in the wrong place, you can of course make the text look rather silly.

1.3 The full stop as an abbreviation mark
Full stops are also used as abbreviation marks, although nowadays many writers do not follow this usage. Hence you may find either:

| Wm. Shakespeare | *or* | Wm Shakespeare |
| J.B. Priestley | | J B Priestley |

Dr. Jekyll and Mr. Hyde *or*	Dr Jekyll and Mr Hyde
Alan Matthews O.B.E.	Alan Matthews OBE
T.V.	TV
R.S.V.P.	RSVP
Jones and Co. Ltd.	Jones and Co Ltd
U.K., U.S.A., and	UK, USA, and
U.S.S.R.	USSR
12 Feb. 1992	12 Feb 1992
A.D. and B.C.	AD and BC
i.e. and e.g.	ie and eg

There are still some exceptions to this optional approach to full stops. Full stops are *never* used for decimal currency (£ and p) or for metric measurements (km, m, cm, kg, g, l, etc).

1.4 The full stop to indicate ellipsis

Finally, a succession of full stops (sometimes called omission marks) is used to indicate ellipsis within or at the end of a sentence, to suggest that something is missing or withheld from a text, or that a sentence is tailing off in an incomplete way. In the latter sense, it may also be used to imply a threat:

(a) What the ... does he think he's talking about?

(b) There was a long, eerie silence and we waited and waited ...

(c) Oh, so you'll hit him, will you? You dare ...

(d) Let us leave them there, murmuring sweet nothings under a waning moon ...

(e) How does it go? 'To be, or not to be, that is the question ...' But I'm afraid I've forgotten the next line.

(f) I promise to tell the truth, the whole truth and nothing but ... so help me.

In (e) and (f) we see ellipsis used to indicate an incomplete quotation – a common context in which to find omission marks.

Generally, we use three dots to indicate the omission of a word or words. If this omission occurs at the end of a sentence, one of these three dots is seen as representing the full stop).

Punctuation Check-up

Make the following texts into sentences, with capital letters at the beginning and full stops at the end. Check your answers with page 87 for accuracy.

(a) the crocodile lives in the mudbanks of rivers in India and Africa his huge body grows to a length of about ten metres people sometimes hunt him for his leather skin he has four short legs and can walk reasonably well but water is his chosen element here he can move really fast

(b) one night a great storm broke over the city the thunder rolled and roared the lightning flashed and the rain fell in torrents everyone stayed indoors and hid from the elements suddenly there was a positive eruption of noise and flashes of blinding light the bursts came again and yet again the huddled masses trembled in their hovels

(c) you have heard of the famous Niagara Falls several men have tried to go over these falls in barrels or small boats in nearly every case the barrels were smashed to pieces against the rocks and the men in them killed or drowned the only man who ever succeeded in going over the falls was Captain Webb later he was to lose his life trying to swim the rapids just below the falls

2

The Exclamation Mark and The Question Mark

In Chapter 1 we said that sentences ended with a full stop *or its equivalent*. There are two modifications of the full stop which may also be used to end a sentence: the exclamation mark and the question mark. They are in fact specialized forms of the full stop, so it would be quite correct to write any of the following sentence variations:

This is a dead parrot.
This is a dead parrot!
This is a dead parrot?
There is a ghost in the bedroom.
There is a ghost in the bedroom!
There is a ghost in the bedroom?

Only the punctuation marks at the end of these sentences tell you which one is a statement, which an exclamation and which a question. Only the punctuation tells you what tone or expression to use if you are reading these sentences aloud (for example, from a playscript). Exclamation marks and question marks signal particular kinds of statement or utterance, and I have listed the main types below.

2.1 The exclamation mark as a signal of emphasis

The exclamation mark is used to signal an exclamation, or emphatic utterance, and often suggests strong emotion. Sometimes it implies a sentence that is not to be taken seriously. The utterances may be complete or incomplete, single words or long sentences, as in:

Heavens above!
Not on your life!
Encore! Encore!

How dare you say a thing like that to me!
What an ass!
How lovely she looked!
Hail, Caesar!
Help!
Look out!

Two tendencies are to be avoided here. One is the gushing
tendency – the addition of exclamation marks to ordinary
statements, perhaps with the intention of artificially
brightening up one's writing, as in:

It was lovely to see you all last week!
Your hospitality was much appreciated!

These two sentences should of course close with a full stop,
and the exclamation marks might in fact be construed as a
gratuitous form of ambiguity. Was it *really* lovely to see them
all last week, one wonders? And was the hospitality perhaps
on the meagre side?

The other tendency to curb is the multiple exclamation
mark which is also used as a rather feeble attempt at extra
emphasis. (There is more on this at **2.3**, *below*.)

2.2 The critical exclamation mark or question mark

You will occasionally come across an exclamation mark or
question mark in parentheses. This rather special use is to
draw attention to something surprising or suspicious or
uncertain in a statement. It is used thus:

He said he was enjoying (!) himself, but he didn't look
too good to me sitting there in his hospital bed.
He said in rapid French that his name was Ellis (?) and
that he wanted a meal – something like that.
He gave an interesting series of talks on the poetry of
Geoffrey Chaucer (?1340 – 1400) and the paintings of
Hieronymus Bosch (?1450 – 1516).

2.3 The question mark to signal interrogation

The normal use of a question mark is of course to signal the
asking of a question. Thus:

Where are you going?
What on earth are you doing?
How far is it to Rickmansworth station?
Where is he, I wonder?
Have you sent in your tax return for last year?

When these questions are being reported indirectly, the question mark is not required. So:

He asked me where I was going.
She asked me what on earth I was doing.
He asked how far it was to Rickmansworth station.
I wondered where he was.
I am writing to ask whether you have sent in your tax return for last year.

Question marks, like flowers and exclamation marks, seem to invite bad writers to use them in little bunches. So we often see things like this:

* Who the hell does he think he is???
* I was really and truly hopping mad with him!!!

The tabloid press has tended to set a bad example in this. In my view, we do well to avoid this misuse of the simple conventions of punctuation, however indifferently we write. It takes more than multiple punctuation marks to pep up a tired piece of text.

Punctuation Check-up
See if you can replace the numbers in these sentences with the appropriate punctuation marks – full stops, question marks, exclamation marks, etc. The answers are on page 87.

(a) It is a painting by Renoir, isn't it(1)
(b) I'd call it a ghastly mess – just look at it (2)
(c) Where's John's ball (3) Give it back to him at once (4)
(d) 'What's the time (5)' asked John (6)
(e) Have you change for a pound coin please (7)
(f) 'What is truth (8)' asked Jesting Pilate, but did not stop for an answer (9)
(g) Help me (10) I'm drowning (11)

(h) Who is the man in that shop (12) I haven't met him before, have I (13)
(i) Pass on the good news (14) He's won the football pools (15)
(j) She asked me where I'd been for my holidays (16)

3

The Comma

The comma is the second key punctuation point. If the full stop is the most important of the 'heavier' stops, the comma is by far the most important of the 'lighter' stops. It is the commonest and most versatile punctuation mark *inside the sentence*. It has been well described as 'the most ubiquitous, elusive and discretionary of all stops'.

3.1 The comma in lists
One of the easiest uses of the comma is in lists. The lists may be nouns, they may be adjectives, they may be verbs or other parts of speech. The rules are similar. Look at these sentences:

(a) They played football, cricket, tennis and rounders.
(b) France, Italy, Germany and the Benelux countries were the founding members of the European Community.
(c) Nick Faldo, Ian Woosnam, Seve Ballesteros and Steve Richardson were members of the Ryder Cup team.
(d) It was an excellent shopping centre with all the main High Street stores, including Boots, W H Smith, Woolworths, John Lewis, and Marks and Spencer.
(e) A variety of old classic comedy movies was on offer, by stars such as Woody Allen, Buster Keaton, the Marx Brothers, and Laurel and Hardy.
(f) For its antiquity, for its massive size, for its peacefulness and its sheer beauty, the cathedral at Chartres is well worth visiting.

The only real question here is whether or not to put a comma between the last two items in a list – the items joined by *and*. The answer to this knotty problem is: it depends. Sometimes the sense demands one, sometimes not. I have used one in (d), (e) and (f) above, but not in (a), (b) and (c). Why? In (a), (b) and (c) the meaning of the sentences does not require a comma to precede *and*. In (d), on the other hand, if we had written *John Lewis and Marks and Spencer*, without a separating comma, a stranger to Britain's High Streets might have wondered if the store in question was called *John Lewis and Marks and Spencer*, or even wondered if there were stores called, on the one hand, *John Lewis and Marks*, and on the other, *Spencer*. The simple addition of a comma resolves any ambiguity. In (e) too, use of a comma before the final *and* resolves a similar problem.

3.2 Commas between adjectives

Often we use two or more adjectives to describe a noun, as in the following sentences. We treat these as we treat any cumulative list, by separating the elements with a comma:

It was a tall, ugly, post-war municipal building.
She was a grumpy, sinister, long-nosed old witch.
The Grand Old Duke of York presided over a council of his feckless, unruly, warlike barons.

There are occasions, however, when multiple adjectives are not used cumulatively, so are not separated by a comma. If we talk about *the Grand Old Duke* (or *a bright red car*, or *a great big dog*), no comma is required. This is because the two adjectives together convey a single idea rather than two different ones: *grand* and *old* convey a single, affectionate sense (just as *bright* and *great* function in a similar way, as modifiers rather than independent adjectives).

Again, where two or more adjectives are linked by *and*, no comma is necessary. So one might write *a dilapidated, blue and white bus*, or *an old, crumbling and derelict building*.

3.3 Commas in pairs

A pair of commas is often required, and is used in the same way as brackets or dashes. Look at these sentences:

George VI, a great-grandson of Queen Victoria, died in 1952.

His second novel, *An Ice-Cream War*, was a great success.

Please notify us, for our records, of any contracts that have been signed up.

You will observe that, for purposes of the business plan, we intend to group these projects together.

You, Mary, must leave at once.

John, who was ugly, got married to Jane, who was gorgeous.

Mr Hurd, the Foreign Secretary, addressed the U N Security Council last night.

One theory, not mentioned in the report, was that ...

The important thing to remember here is that you need to use *a pair of commas* in these situations, one at the start and the other at the end of the parenthesis or apposition – just like brackets. But whereas writers usually remember to close brackets, they very often forget to 'close' a pair of commas.

3.4 Commas for address
Similarly, when addressing someone, commas are used to mark off the person or persons addressed. Naturally, this use is most frequently found in direct speech:

I put it to you, ladies and gentlemen, that we have earned your undivided and unswerving support.

Now, sir, what can I do for you?

3.5 Commas between clauses, to clarify meaning within a sentence
Look at these sentences:

(a) Mary felt unwell and she went off to bed.
(b) She was sick, and tired of studying punctuation.
(c) She was sick and tired of studying punctuation, and she went off to bed.

When do you need a comma? You need one in (b), because without it you would be tempted to read *sick and tired* as a single chunk of meaning. You need one in (c), a sentence which the reader might otherwise feel goes on and on. But you don't strictly need one after *unwell* in (a), because of continuity of subject.

Sentences containing two contrasting statements usually need a comma, especially if you wish to emphasize the contrast:

> She was a highly intelligent woman, but she seems to have acted stupidly on this occasion.
> He was a clever lad, yet he failed the exam.

It would be wrong to omit the commas in these sentences. In sentences where this sense of contrast is absent, or where there is continuity of subject, the comma becomes unnecessary.

3.6   Commas with inverted word order

For reasons of style, sentences are often inverted and the principal part of the sentence is kept to the end. Such inverted sentences are usually punctuated with commas:

> Soon after she came to live here in 1989, she married Mr Bloggs.
> Immediately she got home, she telephoned the police.
> Because she was suspicious, she refused to attend the meeting.
> Until we paid for his broken window, he refused to speak to us.
> The House of Commons having passed the third reading by a large majority after an animated debate, the bill was sent to the Lords.

3.7   Commas with adverbs and adverbial phrases

The tendency to attach superfluous commas to adverbs and adverbial phrases is one of the worst problems of punctuation. It is certainly the case that one meets futile and fatuous examples of the problem every day of the week. What is the point of the comma in the following sentences?

> * I returned to London, from Liverpool.
> * Fervently, he wished Chelsea would score a goal.
> * He celebrated his fiftieth birthday, in August.
> * The party was in full swing, already.

These sentences need no commas at all, so would be better written without them.

Commas are appropriate in the following sentences, however, either to avoid ambiguity or to convey a precise shade of meaning:

    (a) In the morning, rolls and milk are delivered to the house.
    (b) Outside, the car park had been full for hours.
    (c) Inside, the hall was packed with a capacity audience.
    (d) In the main, force is to be avoided.
    (e) I regard his spelling, by and large, as slovenly.
    (f) We have agreed to differ, for the time being.

Adverbs do not demand a profusion of commas, willy-nilly. However, absence of a comma in (a), (b), (c), and (d) would mislead the eye into reading *morning rolls*, *outside the car park*, *inside the hall*, or *main force*. Such confusion is avoidable by the simple insertion of a comma.

3.8 Commas with *however, meanwhile, nevertheless, etc*

Certain adverbs or adverbial phrases are particularly prone to attract gratuitous commas. These include words like *however, meanwhile, nevertheless, first, finally*, etc. Here too it is unwise to comma off unthinkingly. Look at the following:

    (a) However we may interpret the results, the election has been a very close-run thing.
    (b) However, the excitements of the election are now behind us, and we must get on with the exacting if mundane task of governing the country.
    (c) Election campaigns, however exciting in themselves, are no more than a blip in the democratic process.
    (d) Election campaigns, however, exciting in themselves, are no more than a blip in the democratic process.
    (e) First, see Paris. Second, try and get over to London for a few days if funds permit.

(f) If you've never been there, you should go first to Paris.

(g) I want you to look, first, at the new developments and buildings east of Tower Bridge.

(h) Meanwhile the economy was in deepest recession.

(i) Meanwhile, if the economy doesn't pick up soon, there will be another run on the dollar.

(j) Wall Street nevertheless refuses to panic.

(k) On the contrary, measures are being taken to bolster confidence.

Four uses of *however* are given in (a) to (d): depending on the shade of meaning required, writers must take their choice. There are three varieties of *first* shown in (e), (f) and (g). In (i) the comma belongs not to *meanwhile* but to the subordinate clause *if the economy doesn't pick up soon*, and in (k), it separates *contrary* from *measures*.

3.9 Commas with numbers
For once, the rule here is fairly simple. Use commas to prevent ambiguity:

On August 6, 1945, 70 000 civilians perished in the atomic blast at Hiroshima.

Between 1939 and 1945, 55 000 000 people are believed to have been killed.

On 27 March 1977, 574 people died in the Canary Islands when two planes crashed.

On November 11, men and women remember the dead of two world wars.

Between 1840 and 1860, 3 000 000 Irish people – almost half the population – perished or emigrated.

The tendency to use commas in addresses, as in '10, Downing Street' or '16, Cavendish Place' is now dying out. The commas serve no useful purpose here, and this practice is to be discouraged.

3.10 Commas in complex sentences
Generally speaking, the longer and more complex the sentence, the harder it is to avoid using commas. Study the following sentences and see if you agree that commas are

necessary where I have placed them. It is not so important to devise rules for all of these uses – rather to get a feel for the general principles governing when to use and when not to use commas:

> Napoleon inspected his huge Russian army and, whenever possible, he exhorted his generals to greater efforts.

> Whenever he felt himself overstretched, he delegated authority to these generals, and several of them successfully engineered important, even crucial, military victories.

> If the Russian winter had not been so severe, and his lines of communication could have stretched to it, he would have ruled an empire reaching all the way from the Atlantic to the Pacific Ocean.

> If, when you study Napoleon's Russian strategy, you find a certain resemblance to a similar, 20th-century military campaign, you will appreciate one of the great ironies of modern European history, the fact that two great militarists were defeated by the weather, and by their sheer ignorance of the basics of European geography.

> I wonder whether, if the situation ever arose in the future, a third person would make the mistake of invading Russia before making certain of his ability to complete the campaign successfully ahead of the onset of a grim, chilling, relentless and unforgiving Russian winter.

3.11 The comma to introduce or mark off direct speech

Direct speech is usually introduced by a comma, especially after simple verbs of saying, asking, exclaiming, shouting, etc. Look at these:

> Mrs Evans looked at her neighbour and said with feeling, 'I wish you'd stop talking such nonsense.'

> The voice of the loudspeaker announced ponderously, 'The train now standing at platform 12 is the 6 o'clock Inter-City express to Cardiff.'

> The referee yelled to his linesman, 'Was that player off-side?'

Similarly, a comma is usually found at the end of direct speech which precedes a verb of saying, exclaiming, etc. It also encloses split quotations, as in (c). Look at these:

(a) 'I have no complaints,' she said with a smile.
(b) 'There's no point in pursuing this conversation,' he growled, and walked off. 'Let's forget it then,' replied the girl with a grimace in the direction of his receding back.
(c) 'I'm leaving,' Mary announced with emphasis, 'even if you ask me to stay.'

3.12 The comma to indicate omission

Sometimes a comma is used to show that a word or words have been omitted, especially if the word or words were used earlier in the sentence:

Some savers prefer to invest their money in property; others, in the stock market.

But the comma is not used if the meaning of the sentence is clear without it. So:

She was in love with him and he with her.

3.13 Commas for meaning

We saw that a comma made all the difference between:

She was sick, and tired of studying punctuation.
and
She was sick and tired of studying punctuation.

Look too at these:

(a) They were going to Spain, perhaps with the Browns.
(b) They were going to Spain perhaps, with the Browns.
(c) The castle, rescued from its former dilapidation, is worth a visit.
(d) The castle which overlooks the old town is worth a visit, but the 18th-century ruin down by the port is a bit of a mess.
(e) Soldiers, whose wits are dim, do not survive the first attack.

(f) Soldiers whose wits are dim do not survive the first attack.

In (a) and (b), the important thing is to avoid putting commas on either side of *perhaps*, thereby making the sentence's meaning ambiguous. In (d), we find that there is more than one castle under review. In (e), the writer implies that *all* soldiers are dim-witted, whereas in (f) it is implied that *only* dim-witted soldiers are in danger.

3.14 When to avoid commas

Generally speaking, no comma should come between a subject and its verb. So it is superfluous and wrong to put a comma after *wedding* in this sentence, although we see such a misuse often enough:

* The hat that she wore to the wedding, is the one she bought in Harrods.

Nor do we need the superfluous commas in these sentences:

* She told me, that she would come.
* They left strict instructions, that no one should disturb them.
* I cannot imagine, what she is doing.

We have already pointed out that it is wrong to separate two sentences with a comma. They should only be separated by a full stop. So, in (a) the comma is inadequate, and is quite wrong. A full stop is required, and (b) is right:

(a) * The train at platform 10 is the London train, it leaves in five minutes.
(b) The train at platform 10 is the London train. It leaves in five minutes.

3.15 The wrongly-placed comma

A common error is to misplace a comma. Look at the following:

*He stopped the car, and leaving the engine running, jogged back to the scene of the accident.
* A wicked, and on the face of it, a senseless crime.
* John Donne is mainly remembered for the

metaphysical, even the religious content, of his poetry.
* He found his spectacles, and looking again at the newspaper, re-read the offending article with a grim face.

How should these sentences be punctuated? As follows:

He stopped the car and, leaving the engine running, jogged back to the scene of the accident.
A wicked and, on the face of it, a senseless crime.
John Donne is mainly remembered for the metaphysical, even the religious, content of his poetry.
He found his spectacles and, looking again at the newspaper, re-read the offending article with a grim face.

3.16 The missing comma
We have already noted the tendency towards minimizing punctuation. This sometimes results in false economy and an absence of commas where the sense of the text cries out for punctuation. Look at these:

* A lot of what he said of course was nonsense.
* The English love most animals and above all dogs.
* As the clock ticked on the fuse burned and sputtered noisily.
* As far as I knew that story was apocryphal.
* Where appropriate compensation might have been paid by the insurance company.

In all of these sentences, the reader is led astray by the absence of suitable punctuation. All is made instantly clear by the addition of commas:

A lot of what he said, of course, was nonsense.
The English love most animals and, above all, dogs.
As the clock ticked on, the fuse burned and sputtered noisily.
As far as I knew, that story was apocryphal.
Where appropriate, compensation might have been paid by the insurance company.

Punctuation Check-up

Here are some passages which make little sense without commas and full stops. Add the commas and full stops where you think they are necessary, and check your answers with pages 87 and 88, where the texts are written out with the proper punctuation.

(a) The opening ceremony took place in the presence of the German economics minister the Spanish culture minister the Mayor of Frankfurt the president of the German Publishers' Association and the great and good of the European book trade also present was a gaggle of gregarious writers assorted literary glitterati and of course the ever-watching omnipresent remainder merchants

(b) To make cucumber soup you need one large cucumber one onion two ounces butter one and a half pints white stock seasoning and a quarter pint of thick cream to cook you need to toss the vegetables in the hot butter for a few minutes taking care they do not brown add the stock the piece of cucumber peel and a little seasoning simmer for twenty minutes then emulsify in a liquidizer or sieve cool then blend in the cream

(c) As well as Mass on Sundays and her weekly visits to a wayside dance-hall Bridie went shopping once every month cycling to the town early on a Friday afternoon she bought things for herself material for a dress knitting wool stockings a newspaper and paperbacked Wild West novels for her father she talked in the shops to some of the girls she'd been at school with girls who had married shop-assistants or shop-keepers or had become assistants themselves most of them had families of their own by now they had a tired look most of them from pregnancies and their efforts to organize and control their large families (from *The Ballroom of Romance* by William Trevor)

(d) West of the town centre at 2 De Ruyterlaan is the Natuurmuseum with a collection of rare birds insects reptiles and mammals minterals and fossils nearby stands the Synagogue topped by a somewhat oriental copper dome it dates from 1928 east of here is the Boulevard of the Liberation from which the Langestraat branches off on the left leading into a street called De Klomp on the left-hand side is the Elderinkshuis (1783) the only historic building in the town to survive the Great Fire of 1862

(e) We invited John and Frances for supper and Mary happened to drop in too afterwards we had a long discussion about whether to have a cup of tea or coffee with rum in it in the end David took us all out for a drink he ordered a whisky and lemonade a gin and tonic two dry martinis with ice three cokes a lager and lime and a brandy and soda I'm glad I wasn't footing the bill

4

The Semicolon

In current usage the semicolon occupies a position midway between the full stop and the comma. Stronger than the comma, it is sometimes said to be slightly weaker than the colon. Colons and semicolons have in fact often been used more or less interchangeably and indiscriminately over a period of several hundred years. Some differentiation should however be attempted, and the following two chapters try to achieve this.

The semicolon today is used in lists, or instead of a conjunction or connector.

4.1 The semicolon in lists

In Chapter 3.1, we showed the use of the comma in lists. And indeed, so long as the lists are simple, the comma is the preferred form of punctuation. Hence:

> The garden was a profusion of roses, clematis, lilies, sweet peas, delphiniums, red-hot pokers and dahlias.

But if the items listed can themselves be grouped together, we may use the semicolon. This is especially useful if commas are already in use within the listed items. So:

> There was an alpine garden with sea-pinks, saxifrages, thyme and candytuft; a herbaceous border full of hosta, geum, aquilegia, astilbe, phlox, delphinium and potentilla; and at the far end there was a splendid wall of fuchsia, broom, rhododendron and other flowering shrubs.
>
> The meal was a great success, with a starter of tomato cocktail garnished with mint, lemon and other herbs; followed by a fish pie containing whitefish, bacon and

creamed potatoes; and for dessert, a gâteau with pears, redcurrants, cream and sorbet.

Copies of the report have been faxed to our offices in Lagos, Nigeria; Nairobi, Kenya; and Harare, Zimbabwe.

It is easy to see that the use of commas in these sentences instead of semicolons could confuse the reader.

4.2 The semicolon instead of a conjunction or connector

Semi-colons may also be used to separate clauses, sometimes in order to convey antithesis or opposing ideas (with or without a connector such as *and*, *but*, or *yet*); sometimes merely to compensate for the absence of a connector; or else to avoid the over-use of connectors. Note that connectors such as *also*, *consequently*, *furthermore*, *moreover*, *nevertheless*, *hence* and *however* are often preceded by a semicolon. Look at these examples:

We liked John; we disliked his politics.

As a neighbour, he deserved our courtesy and consideration; as a politician, he provoked our silent scorn.

I will say no more about this matter; the chapter is closed.

You may be sorry; I am delighted.

She may have seemed a good prime minister; yet she signally failed to appreciate the changing circumstances of the country.

Hate her, you may; despise her, you cannot.

The Egyptians were masters of practical geometry; hence the pyramids.

Churchill was a great man; moreover, he had a sense of history.

He was a distinguished academic geographer; he had wide-ranging research skills; he published books in all sorts of subject areas; he was also a devoted husband and father.

Some writers might prefer to use full stops in place of the semicolons in these sentences. Stylistically, the effect of full stops is to separate the parts of these statements further apart than the semicolons do. To do this is slightly to change the meaning of the sentences. For, as Gowers puts it in *Plain Words*, the semicolon here is saying, 'Here is a clause or sentence too closely related to what has gone before to be cut off by a full stop.' Yet again, other writers might prefer to use colons here, instead of semicolons. These writers are guilty of failing to discriminate between two distinguishable parts of speech. For further consideration of these distinctions, you must read the chapter on the colon.

Punctuation Check-up

Here are some sentences which lack semicolons and, in some cases, commas. Try to punctuate them suitably, and then check your results with the answers on page 88. Study the punctuated sentences carefully in order to appreciate the function of the semicolon in them.

(a) This is my umbrella that is yours.

(b) She told us the whole story it seemed to go on and on for hours.

(c) That's not fair I don't think you know the whole story.

(d) I'm afraid I can't find her she must have left the office.

(e) The doctor did her morning rounds of the wards she was accompanied by two nurses a specialist and a physiotherapist.

(f) The judge passed sentence the defendant passed out the press corps sprinted off to relay the news of the verdict to a waiting world.

(g) The chickens had gone perhaps the fox had got in to the hen-house during the night.

5

The Colon

As we noted in the last chapter, the semicolon and the colon both occupy a position roughly midway between the comma and the full stop. They are stronger than the former and milder than the latter, and the semicolon is often said to be a shade weaker than the colon. I would prefer to say that the colon performs slightly different functions from the semicolon, but that both of these punctuation marks carry roughly the same weight.

5.1 The colon used to introduce something or to direct attention

The colon is the preferred punctuation mark for introducing something which explains or illustrates or rephrases a previous statement: a quotation, a list, an idea, a definition, an example, etc. Sometimes this use of the colon is followed by *namely*. Look at these:

(a) The tornado left a trail of indescribable devastation in its wake: buildings reduced to contorted heaps of rubble, trees snapped and tossed about like matchsticks, cars and buses lying around everywhere – often far from any highway.
(b) The following articles were missing from his wallet: two cheque cards, a driving licence, railcard, library tickets, and a photograph.
(c) We need the following items: bread, butter, milk, tea, eggs and a box of matches.
(d) There is one thing I'd really like: namely, a job.
(e) He had only one real pleasure in life: eating.

A special aspect of this use of the colon occurs in books like this, where the colon serves to introduce examples. There are three instances on this page.

It is general practice nowadays not to follow a colon with a capital letter unless you are introducing a specific quotation. See **5.5.**

5.2 The colon used as a balance

The colon is used in sentences where the statement that follows it explains, balances or amplifies the statement that precedes it. Look again at sentence (d) in **5.1.** Other examples of this use are:

Guess what: John has won the football pools.
One thing is certain in all this: the best man doesn't always win.
He can do it: and he will.
Knowledge is one thing: the opportunity to use it is quite another.

5.3 The colon in a title

One special use of the colon is to separate a book title and its subtitle, as in the following:

D H Lawrence: Man and Author
Classics and Commercials: A Literary Chronicle of the Forties
A Friend of Humanity: Selected Short Stories of George Friel

5.4 The colon for ratios

This use of the colon is a straightforward carry-over from mathematical notation. Hence:

Girls outnumbered boys in the proportion 3:2.

5.5 The colon to introduce direct speech and quoted material

Some writers prefer to use the colon instead of the comma to introduce direct speech. So:

He muttered quietly: 'Some people are never happy.'
They sang, in quiet harmony: 'John Brown's body lies a-mouldering in the grave...'

It is, however, preferable to use the comma. If a text is full of dialogue, the use of the colon gives a rather spotty effect. It is also slightly solemn. On the other hand, a colon is better than a comma for introducing a lengthy quotation, as in:

I take my text from Genesis, chapter 2:

5.6   The colon after salutations in letters
The American usage in formal correspondence is to write *Dear Sir*: or *Dear Madam*: or *Ladies and Gentlemen*: current British office practice is to use a comma or no punctuation at all.

Punctuation Check-up
The following sentences are incompletely punctuated: all of them lack a colon and/or some commas. Can you provide each sentence with its missing colon and commas? Check your answers on page 88 and 89. Study each sentence to ensure you are clear about the colon's use.

(a) Work fascinates me I can sit and look at it for hours.

(b) There is a wonderful panoramic view from the top of the hill the Castle the Old Town the spires the monuments and the high rise buildings are all laid out before you.

(c) We climbed four peaks last week Lochnagar and Mount Keen on Friday Ben Avon and Cairngorm on Saturday.

(d) There are all sorts of boats in the harbour yachts catamarans speedboats dinghies fishing boats etc.

(e) That has to be one of the surest signs of oncoming old age when you notice how young policemen have become.

(f) He is exactly what everyone says he is a bore and a fool.

(g) The doctor has told her the worst her husband is not likely to recover.

(h) The following items were stolen a purse a ring cheque cards and a diary.

6

The Apostrophe

The apostrophe is a small punctuation mark that looks like a flying comma. Diminutive as it is, it must be the most abused punctuation mark in English today. From the smallest children insisting on the apostrophizing of every plural in sight; to the leader pages of our 'quality' press; via the visible and often highly-ornate manifestations of signwriters' confusion up and down the land (*Baked Potato'es is a favourite, or *Fish n' Chip's): the confusion seems to be universal. Yet the rules governing the use of the apostrophe are very simple.

6.1 The apostrophe to indicate possession

Possession, or ownership, in English singular nouns is formed by the addition of *s* preceded by the apostrophe mark. In plurals which already have an *s* the apostrophe alone is used. In irregular plurals without *s*, the rule is the same as for the singular. So the apostrophe mark is the sign of ownership or possession. Look at these:

Singular nouns: the lion's mane, Mary's hat, the ship's captain, the knight's shining armour, a busman's holiday, Monday's child, Dick Turpin's horse, etc.
Regular plural nouns: two boys' bikes, two ships' crews, the ladies' golf club, the Mothers' Union, the Strangers' Gallery, ten years' imprisonment, etc.
Irregular plural nouns: the children's toys, the Women's Institute, etc.

A problem associated with this rule is how to indicate the possessive of nouns and proper names ending in *s*: words like hostess, princess, Thomas, James, Keats, Burns, etc. The general rule nowadays is to treat such nouns in the same way as any other singulars and write the hostess's kindness, the princess's children, St Thomas's Hospital, St James's Street, Keats's poetry, etc.

Some writers qualify this general rule, saying that the use of an 's depends upon whether or not a pronounceable final syllable is thus formed; if the syllable is pronounced, the 's is used; if no final pronounceable syllable is formed, the apostrophe is retained but no s is added. So they would write Saint Saens' music, Socrates' philosophy, for righteousness' sake. They would also treat numerous classical and biblical names in this special way: such as Aristophanes, Xerxes, Ulysses, Moses, Jesus.

Note that the apostrophe has entirely dropped out of some – but not all – proper names. Place names which have dropped the apostrophe are St Albans, St Andrews, St Helens, St Neots, Earls Court, Golders Green. Land's End, St Michael's Mount, Lord's Cricket Ground and St John's Wood retain it. An illustration of the trend is given by the village of St Abbs in Berwickshire, which has lost its apostrophe, while the nearby cliffs at St Abb's Head retain theirs.

Another problem occasionally associated with ownership is when a group of nouns is involved (the 'group genitive'). This need not give trouble. Only the last member of the noun group takes the apostrophe. Thus:

> Tom, Dick and Harry's aunt.
> William and Mary's joint and glorious reign.
> *Some Experiences of an Irish RM* is Somerville and Ross's most famous book.

6.2   The apostrophe to indicate time or quantity
This is really just a simple modification of **6.1**. It is found in expressions such as *in a week's time*, *my money's worth*, etc, indicating a form of possession.

6.3   The apostrophe to indicate omission of letters
The apostrophe is often used to indicate that one or more letters have been deleted from a word, or that two words have been pushed together. Thus:

I am	> I'm	
cannot	> can't	
do not	> don't	
that will do	> that'll do	
it was	> 'twas	
influenza	> 'flu	> flu
omnibus	> 'bus	> bus
telephone	> 'phone	> phone
aeroplane	> 'plane	> plane

Note the last 4 words, which used the apostrophe for a period of their development and have now dropped it completely.

Other common shortened forms are *I've, you've, we've, they've, I'll, you'll, we'll, they'll, you're, we're, they're, won't, can't, mustn't, oughtn't, shouldn't, didn't, he's, she's*. The word *it's* needs a special comment. It always indicates a shortened version of *it is*, never a possessive pronoun. The possessive pronouns – *mine, yours, his, hers, its, theirs* – do not use the apostrophe, with the single exception of *one's*. So:

It's a nice day = It is a nice day.
His painting is more valuable than yours or hers, but theirs is the most valuable item in the entire collection.
The poor dog pined for its master for fourteen long years. Its story has captured the hearts of children for over a hundred years.
Indeed it's quite a sad and touching tale.

One or two other words spelt with an apostrophe show omission:

ne'er-do-well	> never
one o'clock	> of the
will o'the wisp	> of

It is perhaps interesting to note in passing that the apostrophe to indicate possession originally marked the omission of the letter *e*. So in the Middle English of Chaucer's time, we wrote *the foxes hole, Jameses book, the Knightes Tales, the Wifes Tale of Bath* (>*the Wife of Bath's Tale*).

6.4 The apostrophe to indicate plurals

The apostrophe is sometimes used to indicate a plural in contexts such as the following:

(a) In the 1980's there was dreadful unemployment in Britain.
(b) There are 650 MP's in the House of Commons.
(c) How many l's are there in parallel?
(d) Before 1789, France was ruled by sixteen Louis's, four Henry's and two Francis's.

Current practice would be to drop the apostrophes in (a) and (b) *above*, and write 1980s and MPs.

6.5 The apostrophe to show abbreviated dates

Sometimes you will see foreshortened dates, as in:

Lord Nithsdale was sentenced to death for his complicity in the '45 Rebellion.
He lived in Paris in '68 at the time of the student riots.
He was present at the fall of Singapore in '41.

This usage is particularly common in connection with political upheavals and military campaigns.

6.6 The apostrophe to indicate non-standard English

The apostrophe is often found in the literary representation of non-standard English. Thus:

A man's a man for a'that.   (Robert Burns)
Youk'n hide de fier, but w'at you gwine do wid de smoke?   (Joel Chandler Harris)

Punctuation Check-up

Make a note of all the words needing apostrophes in the following sentences. Some will be apostrophes for ownership, some will indicate contractions. Check your answers with the list on page 89.

(a) I cant help it if youve already lost money on the purchase.
(b) Its not fair to blame Rita for the accident. Shes had a very hard time recently. Im sure Johns also had a hand in the business.

31

(c) The cars brakes are very squeaky. Itll need to go to the garage.

(d) After the accident, the trains driver was arrested. Im afraid hed been drinking.

(e) Its a bit ridiculous to me, but babies early speech patterns are now the subject of careful academic study. Whats your opinion?

(f) Womens clothes are a lot less conservative than mens – or so Im told.

(g) It was a full days walk back to the campsite, and wed just about had enough.

(h) The firms export business is thriving and theyve just won a Queens Export Award.

(i) Marks new car is a Maxi and his dads got his old Mini, so everyones happy,

(j) The schools library annex was badly damaged by the vandals mindless rampaging. Its a great pity that a few thugs can cause such havoc.

7

Capital Letters

The main uses of the capital letter can be categorized as relating either to punctuation or to proper names. I have tried to summarize the main conventions below. The important thing here, as elsewhere, is to be consistent.

7.1 The capital after a full stop
It is well known that a full stop (or an exclamation mark or a question mark) is used to indicate the end of a sentence. It is an equally widely-recognized convention that every sentence has to begin with a capital letter. So:

> She is a clever woman. What is her name? And where does she come from?
> That was no lady! That was my aunt!

7.2 Capitals after other punctuation marks
Very occasionally, capitals are used after other punctuation marks – for example after a comma to introduce a very direct thought, or after a colon to introduce a quotation. Thus:

> She was thinking, Tomorrow morning I shall know my fate.
> Pope put it nicely: To err is human, to forgive divine.

7.3 Capitals used in a rhetorical context
The exclamation O, or Oh, is nearly always capitalized:

> Help us, O God, to do the right.
> Tell me, O my son, what troubles your restless spirit.

7.4 The first person singular
The only pronoun in English that is invariably written with a capital letter is: I. Thus:

> I am that I am.

7.5 Capitals used to indicate a title

Literary titles (and subtitles) of books, films or plays are always given capitals in English, as in Gibbon's *Decline and Fall of the Roman Empire*, *Whitaker's Almanac*, *The Merchant of Venice*, *The Oxford Companion to Sport*, etc.

This convention is not confined to literary titles, but also applies to ranks, public bodies, names of pubs, etc. So the following all require a liberal application of capital letters: the General Secretary of the Transport and General Workers Union, the President of the National Union of Mineworkers, the Colonel of the 18th Infantry Brigade. However, note carefully the difference between general terms for jobs, which do not require capitals, and specific titles which do. Consider the following:

> She served for many years as secretary to the General Secretary of the Transport and General Workers Union.
>
> He was promoted to the rank of colonel in 1991 and transferred as Colonel-in-chief to the 18th Infantry Brigade.
>
> He was well known as the landlord of the Rover's Return.

7.6 Capitals used in a religious context

Capital letters are used to refer to God, the Holy Spirit, Jesus Christ the Redeemer – the Son of Man, Mary the Mother of God, the Prophet Muhammad. The Bible and its books, the New Testament, the Apocrypha, the Holy Koran, and other scriptures are also given capitals.

7.7 Capitals for days of the week and months of the year

Capitals are always used for the seven days of the week and for the twelve months of the year. They are also used for other special calendar days – Christmas, Easter, Ramadan, Passover, Lent, Shrove Tuesday, Diwali, Good Friday, Yom Kippur, Hanukka, Lammas, etc.

7.8 Capitals for proper names

All proper names – of people, places, historical events, etc – take a capital letter. So:

(a) We sailed to Holland via Hull and Rotterdam.
(b) The Treaty of Versailles was supposed to conclude the First World War, but in fact it planted the seeds of the Second.
(c) We watched President Yeltsin and Prime Minister Major emerge from the meeting an hour ago. Several other presidents and prime ministers remained in the meeting.
(d) A nightingale sings in Berkeley Square, they used to say; nowadays in London squares the wildlife doesn't even cough.
(e) The inventor of the steam engine was a Scotsman, James Watt.
(f) It is a small street running into Fleet Street.
(g) I talked about commas in Chapter Three; there will be more to say about them in later chapters.
(h) I must ask Mum and Dad about that; they must be among the best-informed mums and dads in the world.

The rule to remember here is that we use a capital letter for the particular (*my* Mum and Dad) and a small letter for the general (mums and dads): look at (c), (d), (f), (g) and (h) for examples of this.

Adjectives relating to proper names also need capitals, so:

The visiting Australian cricketers played an excellent Yorkshire eleven.
They were an intellectual Marxist organization and they met monthly in some former Baptist church hall near the bus station.

This rule is not invariable, and you get terms like Yorkshire pudding, Welsh rarebit and Russian roulette retaining their capitals; while other terms like india-rubber tyres, wellington boots, venetian blinds, brussels sprouts and french windows are deemed to have effectively lost their local or personal association and thus have lost their capitals.

Similarly, some proper nouns have become so frequently used that they have become common nouns, and in the process they have lost their capital letter. The trend is noticeable with trade names such as hoover and cola; or with products named from a place, such as cashmere; or with units of scientific measurement named after scientific pioneers, such as watts, joules, amperes or amps, etc. Proprietary names tend to hold on to their capital letter until they become used as a general term for a whole class of product: but we still talk about a Kodak camera, a Bendix engine, a game of Scrabble, etc.

Honorific titles joined to proper names also require capital letters: Her Majesty Queen Elizabeth the Queen Mother, King George the Sixth, the Right Honourable Mr (later Sir) Harold Wilson, Lord and Lady Greensleeves, His Grace the Bishop of Durham, the Provost of Trinity College Dublin, Lord Lyon King-of-Arms, etc. Epithets too require capitals, as in William the Conqueror, Eric the Red, Alfred the Great, John the Baptist, the Iron Duke, etc.

7.9 Capitals for abbreviation
Various countries and political groupings are nowadays written in full capitals (without stops), thus: EC, UK, UN, USA. This tendency also extends to academic institutions, international agencies, and certain companies, for example ICI, IBM, BP, MIT, UNESCO, UNICEF, UNCTAD.

7.10 Capitals and geographical labels
We capitalize north, south, east, and west if they are part of the name of a country or political division or continental area, for example South Africa, Northern Ireland, Western Australia, East Anglia; but otherwise we write eastern Iceland, south-east France, west Edinburgh. Similarly with rivers, mountains, etc. So the River Danube, but the rivers of Europe; Mount Everest but the mountains of North Africa.

7.11 Capitals in poetry
Traditionally, each new line of a poem started with a capital letter, whether or not the punctuation required it. Thus:

> The bustle in a house
> The morning after death
> Is solemnest of industries
> Enacted upon earth ...　　　　　　　(Emily Dickinson)

This rule is no longer invariable, and the printer defers to the typographical preferences of the individual poet.

7.12 Capitals for personifications

Another traditional poetic use of capitals is in the representation of abstractions and personifications. Thus:

> To Mercy, Pity, Peace, and Love,
> All pray in their distress ...
> (William Blake)

Punctuation Check-up

Capital letters and full stops have been left out of these sentences. See if you can re-write them properly. Answers on pages 89-90.

(a) im reading *murder on the orient express* by agatha christie it has to be returned to the library by the end of september

(b) the english cricket team will visit pakistan briefly in december on their way back from australia

(c) will the bbc or itv cover the arsenal v crystal palace game on saturday

(d) im afraid im no expert on french or spanish literature you should speak to professor healey he teaches french and his wife is from argentina i think

(e) in our geography classes, they used to tell us that america was the land of opportunity and britain was the workshop of the world and the nile delta was the breadbasket of egypt

(f) admiral nelson was killed at the battle of trafalgar and sir john moore fell at corunna

(g) the 24 bus goes up whitehall and tottenham court road to camden town and thence to belsize park and hampstead but yesterday there was a diversion because of a tuc procession along euston road

(h) the gaelic language is still spoken today in parts of scotland, ireland, wales and britanny, but it has completely died out in cornwall and on the isle of man

8

The Hyphen

The hyphen is used in two contexts: firstly, in the compounding of words (as in *I had a long-standing agreement with my mother-in-law*); and secondly, in the division of words at the end of a line of print to show that the last word has been broken into two. There are rules and conventions relating to both contexts, but as is usual with aspects of punctuation, they are flexible and are dictated mainly by usage, common sense and careful observation.

8.1 The hyphen in compound words

The use of a hyphen often signals a stage in the fusion of two words. Sometimes these two words can function independently, as with *news + agent >news-agent > newsagent*. Compounds which have gone the distance, as it were, and are now fused hyphenless words include:

bandwagon	fairyland	manpower
battlefield	foodstuffs	mantelpiece
bedroom	football	maybe
blackberry	freshwater *(adj)*	midday
bookcase	gatecrasher	nowadays
breakfast	grindstone	offshoot
breakthrough	hairdresser	onset
bricklayer	handbag	outlook
childbirth	headquarters	postman
clergyman	horsepower	schoolgirl
coalfield	keynote	seaport
downhill	ladylike	seaweed
everyday *(adj)*	landlord	smallpox
everything	layout	sportsman
everywhere	livestock	stepfather

superman	textbook	waistcoat
teapot	torchlight	waterfall
teaspoon	upstairs	wheelbarrow

Compound words which remain – for whatever reason – at the hyphened stage include the following:

able-bodied	hanger-on	S-bend
attorney-at-law	has-been	shock-absorber
bull's-eye	heart-throb	spin-off
court-martial	heart-to-heart	sword-dance
down-and-out	labour-saving	tick-tock
engine-driver	long-standing	time-exposure
father-in-law	make-believe	two-faced
first-class *(adj)*	mid-air	up-and-coming
foot-and-mouth	ne'er-do-well	U-turn
disease	passer-by	wash-basin
good-for-nothing	rag-bag	X-ray

In this category must be included the compound numerals between 21 and 99: *twenty-seven*, *thirty-two*, etc. (But not *six hundred*, *two thousand*, etc.) The other numbers requiring a hyphen are the fractions: *three-quarters*, *one-third*, etc.

Even if you compare dictionary spellings, you will find there are many words in which hyphenation usage varies. In general, a compound noun is written as two words when the first word simply qualifies the second, but as a single hyphenless word if it is well-established, frequently used, and made up of two short one-syllable words: *bedroom, bloodshed, teaspoon*. A hyphen is often preferred in longer, multi-syllable words, or if the absence of a hyphen yields an odd spelling: *Invernessshire, infrared, timeexposure*.

As far as adjectives are concerned, we tend to hyphenate those comprising:

noun/adjective + present participle: long-lasting effect, a wheat-growing programme;
noun + past participle: a rice-based diet, a disease-ridden animal;
adjective + noun: high-frequency occurrences, long-syllable types;

a phrase: a word-for-word account, an all-or-nothing effort, a couldn't-care-less attitude, a never-to-be-forgotten experience, a run-of-the-mill job.

Adjectival compounds should also be hyphenated if they begin with:

> *self-* : self-evident truths, self-sufficient behaviour;
> *well-* : well-defined lines, well-known sportsmen;
> *a number*: a nine-man junta, a three-pronged attack, a ten-year lease, a fifth-form pupil, nineteenth-century poetry.

The 'rules' of these words are as much an aspect of spelling and etymology as of punctuation. By observation, by instinct and by common sense we develop a notion of what is right, and what is wrong. These should prevent us writing expressions like the following:

> *a long standing Member of Parliament; a grand daughter of eleven; a sick berth orderly; a little expected breakthrough; a fair skinned Swedish gentleman; egg laying hens; a low scoring cricket match; a shoulder high catch; a hill climbing fanatic; etc.

And it is important to be careful to hyphenate everything that requires a hyphen: *an anti-whale killing campaign* is presumably the opposite of *an anti-whale-killing campaign*! And *a class of ten year-old girls* is a very different prospect from *a class of ten-year-old girls*. More of this in **8.2**.

8.2 Hyphens with prefixes
Hyphens should be used when the prefixed element:

> *is a proper noun*: pro-Russian, proto-Germanic, post-Classicism, pre-Raphaelite;
> *is a number*: pre-1200 oral literature;
> *is an abbreviation*: non-EC countries;
> *comprises more than one word*: non-syllable-timed languages.

Hyphens must also be used to clarify potentially ambiguous

readings: *He resigned from the football team but was soon persuaded to re-sign for a handsome fee.* Other examples include:

re-form (constitute again) and reform (improve)
re-cover (a chair) and recover (get well)
re-count (votes) and recount (a story)
re-bound (given a new binding) and rebound (bounce back)

Hyphens may also be used to avoid sequences of the same vowel: *co-operate, re-emphasize, re-educate, pre-eminent,* etc.

8.3   English proper nouns with a hyphen

Places such as Berwick-upon-Tweed, Burton-on-Trent, Grantown-on-Spey, Newcastle-upon-Tyne, Southend-on-Sea, Stow-on-the-Wold, Stratford-on-Avon, Weston-super-Mare are written with a hyphen.

Most English double-barrel names require a hyphen, as in Sir Alec Douglas-Home, Lady Elizabeth Bowes-Lyon, Vita Sackville-West, David Ormsby-Gore, Antony Armstrong-Jones, etc.

8.4   The hyphen to indicate word breaks

Traditionally, compositors and typesetters were trained in the division of words, and had some appreciation of what was permissible and what was not. Now that we all have word processors, and are all typesetters of sorts, these very sensible conventions have been largely forgotten and our newspapers and other print sources daily assail us with all sorts of typographical horrors. They are horrors because they can completely interrupt our reading at speed – often we have to go back and re-read something (maybe even more than once) before we can sort it out. Everyone will be able to supply their own favourite examples, but breaks to avoid include items like the following:

*bre-akfast	*reap-pear
*ex-acting	*rein-stall
*fin-ding	*screwd-river
*he-ating	*the-rapist
*leg-ends	*unself-conscious
*miss-hapen	

The reason for not dividing words in this way is self-evident: the results confuse the reader, however briefly.

A word may generally be divided after a vowel, taking the next consonant over to the following line, so *hy-phen, persecu-tion, meta-physician, metaphy-sician, metaphysi-cian, ve-getation, vege-tation, vegeta-tion,* are all acceptable breaks. In participles, break the word at *-ing*, thus *giv-ing, break-ing, enter-ing,* but *run-ning, chuck-ling,* etc. It is also generally possible to divide words between two successive consonants or vowels, thus *univer-sity, cor-puscles, syl-lable, perfor-mance, ad-dress, appreci-ate,* etc. But letters that influence the pronunciation of another letter should not be separated at line breaks, so *spe-cial, magi-cian, Gre-cian, ascen-sion.*

Perhaps the best rule in this area is to avoid word division if possible. Many good word processors are wisely programmed to do just that.

8.5 Special effects
Sometimes the hyphen is used to separate the letters of words for a special reason. For example:

> I'm very hard of hearing. Please speak to me very s-l-o-w-l-y and c-l-e-a-r-l-y.
> 'I'll b-b-break your b-b-bloody neck,' he stuttered furiously.

Punctuation Check-up
Here are some not-terribly-serious texts which are rather short of hyphens. Can you supply the missing hyphens, where appropriate? Check your answers with page 90, where the hyphenated words are set out.

(a) In the country of the blind, the one eyed man is king. (one hyphen)

(b) Mr Mouse fell off the table; what did Mrs Mouse do? She gave him mouse to mouse resuscitation. (two hyphens)

(c) There was a two hundred strong search party of policemen backed up by thirty odd tracker dogs. (three hyphens)

(d) Guess what happened to my shockproof, corrosion resistant, anti magnetic, waterproof pocket calculator? It caught fire! (two hyphens)

(e) In their warm up game the visitors impressed in several departments: the scrum half and stand off combination had the opposition running all over the place with their mid run dummies and kicks of hair raising accuracy, while the full back's up and unders kept them pinned well back in the cul de sac of their own half. The half time whistle didn't come a moment too soon. (eleven hyphens)

(f) The conference was a very made up affair of off the peg socialism and back of the envelope idealism. The make up men had a field day, as did the ice cream men at the entrance to the hall. Nobody paid the slightest attention to the out patients department across the carpark. (nine hyphens)

(g) My mother in law Mrs Mary Rose Fotherington Thomas from Henley on Thames is a very long standing dyed in the wool Conservative member of the local community council. Currently active in an anti drugs campaign, she is an extremely sprightly and able bodied eighty seven year old, often to be seen driving along Henley Main Street at breakneck speed. The first time we met was at a little frequented local beauty spot – the week after I had made the breakthrough and proposed to her daughter. (sixteen hyphens)

(h) Prominent at last night's meeting were the vice chancellor of the university, the ex president of the students' union, the non executive chairperson of the schools' liaison committee, and the acting director of the main fund raising event of this year's Charities Week. They agreed to try for a two thirds increase in student participation this year. (five hyphens)

9

Quotation Marks and Direct Speech

Quotation marks, or quotes, are sometimes called inverted commas, because that is what they look like. They come in pairs, like brackets – one to open and one to close the quotation. Their main functions are:

1. to mark off direct speech:
   'I'm afraid there's been an accident,' he shouted into the telephone. 'Can you send someone to help us?'
   'Are there any wounded?' asked the voice at the other end of the line.

2. to show that a word or phrase is highlighted or used as if it is being quoted:
   What is the meaning of 'euphemistic'?
   He called me 'a wolf in sheep's clothing' – whatever he meant by that.

3. in traditional handwritten texts, to indicate a title (but *see* also **9.5**):
   Last night we saw an excellent performance of 'West Side Story' at the King's Theatre.
   She's been trying to read 'War and Peace' for the last six months.

9.1 Direct speech

If you want to use quotation marks to signal direct speech, you must use them only to enclose the speaker's actual words and not a reported version of those words. It is a common error to put quotes round reported speech. For example:

(a) *The prime minister explained that 'it was foolish to look for scapegoats in such tragic circumstances. It is much more important to ascertain the precise cause of the accident and take whatever steps are necessary to ensure that it never happens again.'

(b) *She timidly asked 'if he still planned to go home tomorrow?'

(c) *The press were good enough to describe me as 'one of my country's best ambassadors', which was very kind of them.

In (a) the prime minister would not have said 'It *was* foolish ...' but would almost certainly have said 'It *is* foolish ...' So the opening quotation mark should be moved to the beginning of the next sentence. In (b) and (c) too, it is not the actual words that are quoted. They could be rewritten in the following ways:

She timidly asked if he still planned to go home the following day. (Reported speech)
She timidly asked him, 'Do you still plan to go home tomorrow?' (Direct speech)
The press were good enough to describe me as one of my country's best ambassadors, which was very kind of them. (Reported speech)

The original versions of these sentences are all examples of a bad practice: the mixing up of direct and reported speech. It is important to be consistent to the mode you select, and to realize that the conventions for direct speech are not the same as those which apply to reported speech. Here are two versions of the same longer passage, the first using direct speech (Text A) and the second using indirect speech (Text B). Study the differences between them:

Text A

'Girl number twenty', said Mr Gradgrind, squarely pointing with his square forefinger, 'I don't know that girl. Who is that girl?'

'Sissy Jupe, sir,' explained number twenty, blushing, standing up and curtseying.

'Sissy is not a name,' said Mr Gradgrind. 'Don't call yourself Sissy. Call yourself Cecilia.'

'It's father as calls me Sissy, sir,' returned the young girl in a trembling voice, and with another curtsey.

'Then he has no business to do it,' said Mr

Gradgrind. 'Tell him he mustn't. Cecilia Jupe. Let me see. What is your father?'

'He belongs to the horse-riding, if you please, sir.'

Mr Gradgrind frowned, and waved off the objectionable calling with his hand.

'We don't want to know anything about that, here. You mustn't tell us about that, here. Your father breaks horses, don't he?'

'If you please, sir, when they can get any to break, they do break horses in the ring, sir.'

'You mustn't tell us about the ring, here. Very well, then. Describe your father as a horsebreaker. He doctors sick horses, I dare say?'

'Oh yes, sir.'

'Very well, then. He is a veterinary surgeon, a farrier, a horsebreaker. Give me your definition of a horse.'

(Sissy Jupe thrown into the greatest alarm by this demand.)

(from *Hard Times*, by Charles Dickens)

Text B

Mr Gradgrind hesitated at the twentieth girl, pointed at her with his square forefinger, and asked her name. When the girl had blushed, stood up, curtseyed, and had given her name as Sissy Jupe, Mr Gradgrind opined that Sissy was not a name and ordered her to call herself Cecilia. In a trembling voice and with another curtsey, the girl replied that it was her father who called her Sissy. Mr Gradgrind was not having any of that, repeating that her name was Cecilia Jupe, and then asking the girl what her father was. The girl explained that her father belonged to the horse-riding, and Mr Gradgrind frowned, waving off the objectionable calling with his hand and assuring her that they didn't want to know anything about that *there*, in the schoolroom. Once it had been established, after further questions, that Mr Jupe was a horsebreaker and horse doctor, Mr Gradgrind asked the child for her definition of a horse – a question which threw her into the greatest alarm.

Obvious differences in the presentation of these texts are the use of quotation marks and new paragraphs in Text A and their absence in Text B. There are changes in tense between A and B – with present becoming past. The word *here* in Text A becomes *there* in Text B. And so on.

For a further note on the paragraphing of dialogue or Direct Speech, please *see* **10.3**.

9.2 Punctuation in relation to quotation marks

Writers often seek guidance on where to put punctuation marks, such as full stops, commas and question marks, in relation to quotation marks. Most publishers now ask writers of text to place commas or full stops before the final or closing quotation mark. (This is, incidentally, the standard American practice – *see* **16.3**.) We need to amplify this advice and say that punctuation marks that belong to, or are part of, the quoted material should be kept within the quotation marks, while other punctuation marks are kept outside the quotes. For example:

I said to her, 'I beg your pardon?'
Why did you say to her, 'I beg your pardon'?

Note carefully the position of the question mark in these two examples.

9.3 Single quotes or double quotes?

Another area of debate is whether to use double (" ") or single (' ') quotation marks. British English tends to favour single. Quotation within quotation is signalled by the use of double quotes. Thus:

'Next week we shall examine the "stream of consciousness" technique in greater detail,' the tutor announced. (British English)

American English generally prefers to use double quotes, keeping single quotes to indicate a quotation within a quotation; for an example of this *see* **16.3**.

There is one clear advantage of the use of double quotes over single quotes. Sometimes – especially with book titles – single quotes are in danger of being confused with apostrophes, as in:

Check your references in 'Whitaker's Almanac' and in the 'Writers' and Artists' Yearbook'.

It is probably ambiguities such as the above, allied with the technological advances offered by word processors, which have encouraged writers to change from putting quotes round titles to underlining them or setting them in italic. For more on this, *see* 9.4 below, and also Chapter 14.

9.4 Highlighting

Quotation marks in this context are a useful way of signalling the special use of a word or phrase, or a change of register:

> We had a delightful meal at the new French restaurant followed by several 'wee drams' back at the house.
> The judge was adamant that the accused man had been extremely 'economical with the truth', so the press immediately branded him as a brazen liar.
> They spoke a very archaic kind of English, full of 'thous' and 'thees' and biblical expressions.

They may also suggest that the writer disagrees with the use of a certain word:

> What he calls a 'dialect' is actually a language with a large grammar and vocabulary of its own.

It is perhaps wise to warn writers against what one reviewer describes as 'over-indulgence in the trick of encasing words or phrases in inverted commas to indicate that they are being used in a slang or technical or facetious or some other unusual sense'. Highlighting may be described as a useful occasional device but a dangerous habit. Too many writers cannot be bothered to seek out the right word, making do with the first ready-made phrases and words that spring into their minds, and drawing attention to their laziness by this use of inverted commas.

9.5 Quotation marks to indicate titles

In modern English handwritten texts such as letters, it is becoming more and more common to underline titles rather than to set them in quotation marks, while the conventions of print are to set them in italics. But the traditional written method of indicating titles of books, articles, poems etc is to put the title in quotation marks. So, as far as general English practice is concerned, the following punctuation is correct:

Although we've seen it before, we wanted to go to see 'West Side Story' at the King's Theatre last night.
Her life is too hectic to permit her to tackle serious reading of long novels like 'War and Peace'.

It is in typesetting and in academic writing that the requirements are more precise. When compiling a bibliography, for example, enclose in quotation marks (do not underline) titles of articles and essays, chapters and sections of books, and unpublished works such as dissertations. Italicize (or underline) titles of published books, plays, pamphlets, periodicals, and classical works (except books of the Bible or other scriptures). Italicize (or underline) titles of poems only if they have been separately published under that title, otherwise enclose titles of poems in quotations.

Thus, for published books (in this case, about the novels and stories of F Scott Fitzgerald):

Kazin, Alfred (ed). *F Scott Fitzgerald: The Man and His Work*. Cleveland: World 1951
Mizener, Arthur. *The Far Side of Paradise*. Boston: Houghton Mifflin 1951

And for articles:

Bewley, Marius. 'Scott Fitzgerald and the Collapse of the American Dream,' in *The Eccentric Design: Form in the Classic American Novel*. New York: Columbia University Press 1959
Geismar, Maxwell. 'F Scott Fitzgerald: Orestes at the Ritz,' in *The Last of the Provincials: The American Novel 1915 – 1925*. Boston: Houghton Mifflin 1943

For more on the use of italics, *see* Chapter 14.

Punctuation Check-up
Write out these sentences with appropriate punctuation –

quotation marks, commas, full stops, question marks, capital letters, etc. Check your sentences with the answers on page 90.

(a) Is this the road to the seashore asked the motorist

(b) Im not sure replied the young lady im a stranger here myself

(c) I told you to buy a map said his wife and now its too late and all the shops are shut.

(d) My favourite reading this year has been the ice cream war a novel by william boyd and muriel grays funny account of her hill-walking experiences which is called the first fifty

(e) I am honoured to receive this award announced the mp and i will always cherish it thank you very much ladies and gentlemen

(f) In the end she said we took the umbrella to the lost property office it was too good an item to simply leave lying in the street she added by way of explanation

(g) The chances of a serious accident began the professor are greater than ever i suppose he went on none of you ever considered the possibility of a nuclear explosion or did you

(h) But this said angela is murder i must phone the police she added her voice growing more shrill

10

The Paragraph

10.1 Organizing of information

Elsewhere we said that the full stop was the strongest punctuation mark in the sentence. It marks the end of a sentence, which we said tries to articulate a complete and unified thought. In a piece of extended writing running to many sentences and several pages, more complex 'thoughts' or topics are given expression. To help the reader process extended pieces of text, writers usually show how they have grouped the sentences into chunks of meaning. This helps the reader to perceive at a glance the broader structure of the text. The writer's means of conveying information about this structure is by paragraphing.

A paragraph may be defined as a sentence or group of sentences dealing with one main idea or topic, or as a short passage with unity of purpose.

Look at the following two texts. At a glance, you would probably say that Text A was more difficult than Text B. Why?

Text A

Long ago there was a Calabar hunter called Effiong who lived in the bush. He killed plenty of animals and made much money. Everyone in the country knew him, and one of his best friends was a man named Okun, who lived near him. Effiong was very extravagant and spent so much money in eating and drinking with people that at last he became quite poor, and he had to go out hunting again. But now his good luck seemed to have left him, for although he worked hard and hunted by day and by night, he completely failed to catch anything. One day, as he was very hungry, he went to his friend Okun and borrowed two hundred rods of money from him. He told Okun to come to his house on a certain day for repayment of this money, and he also told him to bring his gun, loaded, with him.

Text B
Long ago there was a Calabar hunter called Effiong who lived in the bush. He killed plenty of animals and made much money. Everyone in the country knew him, and one of his best friends was a man named Okun, who lived near him.

Effiong was very extravagant and spent so much money in eating and drinking with people that at last he became quite poor, and he had to go out hunting again. But now his good luck seemed to have left him, for although he worked hard and hunted by day and by night, he completely failed to catch anything.

One day, as he was very hungry, he went to his friend Okun and borrowed two hundred rods of money from him. He told Okun to come to his house on a certain day for repayment of this money, and he also told him to bring his gun, loaded, with him.

Text A looks rather formidable. It looks like a rather dense piece of writing, simply because it is unbroken by paragraphs. Text B on the other hand looks easier to read because it *has* been organized into paragraphs.

In a book on punctuation, it is important to remember that the *appearance* of a text is important. A paragraph is just one more visual aid. It signals a stage in the development of a textual argument or discussion.

It is not very useful to fix rules regarding the length of a paragraph. It is far more important to remember that a paragraph is a *unit of thought and not a unit of length*.

10.2 Sequential structure of a text
It is important that your paragraphs encapsulate a unity of thought which the reader can identify. If each new paragraph draws attention to a new topic (or scene or argument), your drift will be clear and coherent. You must not arbitrarily jettison this coherence, for example by

combining into a single paragraph short passages that lack any inherent unity of thought – that will mislead the reader.

Writers used to be trained to build each paragraph around a key sentence. That was the sentence which contained the central idea of the paragraph. And students trying to produce a summary or précis of an extended text were trained to hunt out the key sentences of the paragraphs they had to scan. The key sentence strategy is still a valid one, especially when you are at the planning stages of writing an essay. Your rough list of main topics for the essay may well provide you with a paragraph sequence of key sentences for your finished essay.

Particularly important for a good essay are the introductory paragraph and the last paragraph. The introductory paragraph is where the subject or topic is broached. It offers a statement of the problem, and perhaps some brief comments on the way it is to be treated in the body of the essay. The last paragraph is an opportunity for the essay-writer to sum up the main points covered in the body of the essay, to offer a conclusion and perhaps to express his/ her own views or opinions or decisions.

If you are dealing with fiction, a new paragraph is often called for to indicate a change of speaker (*see* **10.3** below), a change of place, the passage of time, etc.

10.3 Paragraphing for dialogue

In fiction, where much of the text may be in the form of dialogue, the conventions of paragraphing change slightly. You need to start a new paragraph when dialogue is going to begin. Look at the following text and watch how each new speaker is given a new paragraph:

> 'Margaret,' called Mrs Munt, 'is Helen all right?'
>
> 'Oh yes.'
>
> 'She is always going away in the middle of a programme,' said Tibby.
>
> 'The music has evidently moved her deeply,' said Fräulein Mosebach.
>
> 'Excuse me,' said Margaret's young man, who had for some time been preparing a sentence, 'but that lady has, quite inadvertently, taken my umbrella.'

'Oh, good gracious me! – I am so sorry. Tibby, run after Helen.'

'I shall miss the Four Serious Songs if I do.'

'Tibby love, you must go.'

'It isn't of any consequence,' said the young man, in truth a little uneasy about his umbrella.

'But of course it is. Tibby! Tibby!'

Tibby rose to his feet, and wilfully caught his person on the backs of the chairs. By the time he had tipped up the seat and had found his hat, and had deposited his full score in safety, it was 'too late' to go after Helen. The Four Serious Songs had begun, and one could not move during their performance.

'My sister is so careless,' whispered Margaret.

'Not at all,' replied the young man; but his voice was dead and cold.

(From *Howard's End*, by E M Forster.)

For further information on setting out dialogue, please consult the chapter on direct speech (**9.1** and **9.2**).

10.4 Indenting

The mechanics of paragraphing are very simple. You signal a new paragraph in two ways: firstly, by starting a new line; and secondly, by indenting the first word approximately three character spaces in from the left-hand margin. (A recent typographical alternative is to leave a line space between the end of one paragraph and the start of another. If you follow this practice, you do not, additionally, require to indent.)

Punctuation Check-up

Here is a passage of dialogue which has not been set out properly. Can you re-organize it so that each new speaker gets a new paragraph? Check with page 91 afterwards and see if you got it right.

'I wonder who did it?' asked Steve. 'I can't imagine,' answered Lem brokenly. 'Did they get much?' 'All I had in the world ... A little less than thirty dollars.' 'Some smart leather must have gotten it.' 'Leather?'

queried our hero, not understanding the argot of the underworld with which the train boy was familiar. 'Yes, leather – pickpocket. Did anyone talk to you on the train?' 'Only Mr Wellington Mape, a rich young man. He is kin to the Mayor of New York.' 'Who told you that?' 'He did himself.' 'How was he dressed?' asked Steve, whose suspicions were aroused.

(From *A Cool Million*, by Nathanael West.)

Here is another passage from which the paragraphs have been removed. Can you replace them? Check your version with page 91.

At eight o'clock came the doctor. He would allow only a word or two to be uttered, and his visit was brief. Reardon was chiefly anxious to have news of the child, but for this he would have to wait. At ten Amy entered the bedroom. Reardon could not raise himself, but he stretched out his hand and took hers, and gazed eagerly at her. She must have been weeping, he felt sure of that, and there was an expression on her face such as he had never seen there. 'How is Willie?' 'Better, dear, much better.' He still searched her face. 'Ought you to leave him?' 'Hush, you mustn't speak.' Tears broke from her eyes, and Reardon had the conviction that the child was dead. 'The truth, Amy!' She threw herself on her knees by the bedside, and pressed her wet cheek against his hand. 'I am come to nurse you, dear husband,' she said a moment after, standing up again and kissing his forehead. 'I have only you now.'

(From *New Grub Street*, by George Gissing.)

55

11

Brackets

There are various kinds of brackets, including round brackets or parentheses ( ), square brackets [ ], angle brackets ‹›, and brace brackets{ }. In this book, we need only concern ourselves with the first type in any detail, with passing references to the other three types.

11.1 Round brackets (or parentheses)

Round brackets ( ) are sometimes called parentheses, from Greek *parenthesis*, which means literally 'an insertion beside' (here, beside the basic drift of the sentence).

Brackets are a convenient way of marking off subordinate information within a piece of text. Brackets keep the words they enclose out of the way, as it were, so that the reader may concentrate on the main text preceding and following the bracketed material. They are used:

1. to isolate supplementary information (more effectively than commas or dashes), as in:
   Applications for the vacant post (six copies) should be lodged with the Vice-Chancellor by 1 October.
   The result of the election (a 40% swing against the Government) was decisive.
   The result of the election was decisive. (There was a 40% swing against the Government.)

2. to present additional or explanatory (but subordinate) information about details in the text:
   The novels of Neil Gunn (1891 – 1973) and George Friel (1910 – 75) have enjoyed a recent revival of critical interest.

For additonal information, read Chapter 2, especially
section 3 (pages 12 – 15).
Some of the little *bastides* (country houses) of Provence
are completely unspoilt.

3. as an economical way of indicating options:
   Any candidate(s) for the office of Club Secretary must
   be formally proposed and seconded by noon.
   Any speaker(s) will be welcome.

4. for numbers written within a sentence:
   The project has been (1) well funded, (2) carefully
   researched, and (3) brilliantly presented.

The main abuse of brackets in punctuation is if they allow a
writer to wilfully and needlessly interpolate one independent
sentence within another, as in:

   *A fire-drill memorandum (six copies of this
   memorandum are enclosed for members of the Board)
   has been issued to management committees.

This is a completely illegitimate use of brackets. Two
separate sentences are in fact required, each starting with a
capital letter and ending with a full stop.

11.2   Brackets with other punctuation marks

The rules here are simple. A full sentence within brackets,
but standing alone, starts with a capital letter and ends with
a full stop:

   Norma Jean Mortensen took the all-American stage-
   name of Marilyn Monroe. (She might have got
   nowhere under her real name.)

A full sentence incorporated into another sentence starts
with a small letter and does not require a full stop:

   Arthur Anderson (he's the one who makes the funny
   jokes) was in fine fettle.

But such a parenthetical sentence may take a question mark
or exclamation mark:

Mary Bloggs (wait till you see her!) is the name of the new club secretary.

11.3 Square brackets
These are used to enclose letters, words, phrases, comments, corrections, explanations, notes or questions which were not in the original text but have been inserted by later authors or editors:

He [St Stephen] was an early Christian martyr.

The word *sic* (= thus) usually appears in square brackets to confirm that a misspelling or unconventional structure has been left in the text deliberately, and is not to be corrected:

As James Joyce put it: 'My patience are [sic] exhausted.'

11.4 Angle brackets
These only appear in scholarly, text-critical works, where the editor is conjecturally supplying text which is defective, or illegible, or absent from the original source material.

11.5 Brace brackets
These are sometimes referred to as curly brackets, and may be used singly or in pairs. They are employed to signify alternatives, especially in tables.

Punctuation Check-up
Parts of these sentences should go inside round brackets, or parentheses. Can you write them out properly? You may also need to add some commas. Check your answers with those on pages 91-92.

(a) Edward his best friend ignored Roger in the street.
(b) Eileen Crawford a woman I have always admired is coming to our party tomorrow.
(c) We were still are happy to see her settled down in a regular job.
(d) No-one in our house according to my young sister knows how to dress smartly.
(e) The Royal Family pictured left sailed for Norway in Britannia picture on page 3 this afternoon.

(f) He has a wonderful collection of wild flowers anemones primroses and orchids.

(g) Precious metals gold silver platinum etc are best kept locked away in a bank vault.

(h) Edinburgh population 450000 is twice as big as Aberdeen population 220000 and half as big as Dublin population 900000.

(i) We spent 45 francs about £2 sterling on a trip to some amazing underground caves.

(j) He was a complete eccentric ate snails it was said and his every move was closely watched by all his neighbours.

12

The Dash

12.1 The dash – main punctuational uses

The dash – or em rule, as printers call it – is a useful punctuation mark. But because it is much abused – notably by the popular press and by bad letter-writers – many writers are rather afraid to use it at all, which is a pity. Look at the following examples of the valid use of the dash before attempting to summarize the general rules governing the use of this punctuation mark:

(a) Yes – oh dear, yes – the novel tells a story. (*Aspects of the Novel*, by E M Forster)

(b) We know, Mr Weller – we who are men of the world – that a good uniform must work its way with the women, sooner or later. (*The Pickwick Papers*, by Charles Dickens)

(c) There is nothing – absolutely nothing – half so much worth doing as simply messing about in boats. (*The Wind in the Willows*, by Kenneth Grahame)

(d) Many's the long night I've dreamed of cheese – roasted, mostly. (*Treasure Island*, by Robert Louis Stevenson)

(e) Frank Harris is invited to all the great houses in England – once. (attrib. Oscar Wilde)

(f) Advice to persons about to marry – Don't! (*Punch*, 1845)

(g) The English country gentleman galloping after a fox – the unspeakable in full pursuit of the uneatable. (*A Woman of No Importance*, by Oscar Wilde)

(h) But we loved with a love which was more than love – I and my Annabel Lee. (*Annabel Lee*, by Edgar Allan Poe)

(i) She's the sort of woman who lives for others – you can tell the others by their haunted expression. (*The Screwtape Letters*, by C S Lewis)

(j) Go directly – see what she's doing, and tell her she mustn't. (*Punch*, 1872)

(k) The Common Law of England has been laboriously built about a mythical figure – the figure of the 'Reasonable Man'. (A P Herbert)

(l) It is well that war is so terrible – otherwise we would grow too fond of it. (attrib. General Robert E Lee)

There are three main kinds of dash in the above sentences. In (a), (b), and (c) are good examples of the parenthetical dash. Here dashes are used in pairs, and function in the same way as brackets. But the dashes give a slightly stronger – or more abrupt – break than a pair of brackets would provide. Single dashes are used in the remaining sentences – in (d), (e) and (f) for afterthoughts, or for paradoxical or humorous endings to the sentence. Finally, sentences (g) through (l) deploy a single dash so that the second part of the sentence can explain, amplify, paraphrase or correct what has preceded the dash.

A further valid use of the dash is to show where a piece of text has been left unfinished, especially direct speech:

'Well, I'll be –,' he muttered.

'Oh, what a disaster –,' he cried involuntarily.

12.2 The dash – non-punctuational use
Formerly, the dash was often used to signify omission:

Her affair with Lord – was the talk of the town.

We visited the hamlet of M– in the course of our journey.

12.3 The em rule and the en rule
If you have to mark up typescripts for a printer, you will know there are two kinds of dash – the longer, or *em rule*, which we have been discussing - and the shorter, or *en rule*.

(Ems and ens are printers' measures.) The en rule is merely a shorter dash and is used specifically by printers in the following contexts:

1. to indicate a series of ranges:
   the 1914–1918 War
   pages 467–481
   volumes I–IV
   A–Z

2. to combine two words into a compound adjective where neither word modifies the other:
   Indo–Roman archaeology in the Graeco–Roman tradition
   space–time dimensions
   the Sapir–Whorf linguistic hypothesis

Punctuation Check-up

All of these sentences would benefit by the simple addition of one or two dashes. Occasional commas would also help. Can you supply them? Check your answers with page 92.

(a) Walk if you please don't run.

(b) Janice rushed in and rushed out again.

(c) Cars those without permits are only allowed to park for 20 minutes.

(d) I like a good argument a quiet life is so dull.

(e) No-one believes a word he says absolutely no-one at all.

(f) Here's a letter from Nancy what an amazing person she is.

(g) Time we had some decent weather for a change it's been awful this past fortnight.

(h) My great-grandfather on my mother's side of course was said to have been kidnapped by pirates at sea.

(i) Some recent exhibitions have been very successful the Egyptian artefacts for example were visited by half a million people.

(j) It was Saturday afternoon and the streets were empty it was as if the whole population was glued to its television screens indoors.

13

A Note on the Oblique Mark or Slash

Traditionalists might say this is not a punctuation mark at all, and strictly speaking they would perhaps be correct. But the oblique mark, or slash, figures more and more frequently in printed text nowadays, so it seems worth adding a word about its uses. The main uses are:

1. to present text in non-sexist language:
   A writer nowadays is supposed to avoid sexist assumptions. S/he tries to avoid gender references in his/her writing.
   If anyone can offer me a lift to Manchester next Thursday in his/her car, will s/he please telephone me on ...

2. to show alternatives:
   Bring your swimming costume and/or a tennis racquet.
   Tea/coffee will be served.
   Dear Sir/Madam ...
   When the new student arrives, he/she will be introduced to his/her flatmates.

3. as a form of shorthand in advertisements (which is an application of 2):
   Painter/decorator offers free estimates.
   Postgraduate student seeks furnished/unfurnished flat in Marchmont/Meadows/Newington area.
   Beginner/refresher courses in shorthand.

4. to indicate a period of time, especially in a fiscal or academic context:

I was at university in the years 1960/64.
I've just received my 1992/3 tax form.

5. to show the route followed on an itinerary:
   The London/Oxford/Birmingham express was
   derailed at Reading.
   The Edinburgh/Birmingham/Frankfurt flight is
   running half an hour behind schedule.

6. to mark off lines of poetry when they are run on in a text,
   perhaps for reasons of space, instead of being properly set
   out. The oblique mark indicates the line break:
   Fair daffodils, we weep to see/You haste away so soon:/
   As yet the early rising sun/Has not attain'd his noon.

7. as an abbreviation, in certain specific contexts:
   He lives c/o Brown, 16 Cavendish Place. (c/o = care of)
   Charge it to his a/c (a/c = account)
   Major Bateman is the officer i/c provisions. (i/c = in
   charge of)

8. as an abbreviation for *per*, as in:
   90 km/hr, 20 ft/sec

The following passage from the novel *Metroland* (by Julian
Barnes) fits none of these categories exactly, though there are
perhaps elements of 6 in it:

> I suppose I must be grown-up now. Or would 'adult' be
> a better word, a more ... adult word? If you came and
> inventoried me, I'd have ticks in all the appropriate
> boxes. I'm surprised how well camouflaged I seem.
> Age : Thirty/Married : Yes/Children : One/Job : One/
> House : Yes/With mortgage : Yes/(Rock solid so far)/
> Car : Arguable/Jury service : Once, finding accused
> not guilty after long discussion of 'reasonable doubt'/
> Pets : No, because they mess up/Foreign holidays :
> Yes/Prospects : Bloody better be/Happiness : Oh, yes;
> and if not now, then never.

Passages like this are virtuoso performances, and not

perhaps to be held up as a model. On the other hand, they tell us that the oblique has now been truly discovered for its punctuational potential and that writers do make regular use of it. In other words, it's not going to go away.

Punctuation Check-up

Below are some sentences which use sexist language. Try rewriting them by using *s/he*, *his/her*, etc. (You could of course also use plurals, but that would not be a 'punctuational' solution to the problem.) Compare your results with those suggested on page 92.

(a) A student must attempt 3 questions in this exam. He should not spend more than 30 minutes on any single question, and he should ensure that his answers avoid digressions. Marks are allotted on a scale of A to F, with E and F as fail marks. No student will be deemed to have passed the exam if he scores F on any question.

(b) The individual is described in terms of his perception of other members of the group. What is his basic position in the group? How far does he belong to the group that is influencing him? What is his overall attitude to the group?

14

A Note on Using Italics

The use of italics is not strictly a part of punctuation, but it is an important aspect of the overall presentation of text to which passing reference has already been made. It is perhaps useful therefore to summarize here the contexts in which it is usual to italicize print.

14.1 Titles of books, films, works of art, etc

Books, newspapers, magazines, films, plays and works of art are printed in italic. So too are musical works if they are given a special title, but not if they are merely identified by the nature of the musical form in which they are written. Thus:

> Milton's *Paradise Lost* and Shakespeare's *Macbeth*;
> *Treasure Island*, Chapter 3, 'The Black Spot';
> a subscription to the *National Geographic Magazine*
> the *Daily Express*;
> a French comedy film called *Monsieur Hulot's Holiday;*
> Handel's *Messiah* and Beethoven's Fifth Symphony

There are various exceptions to the above generalizations. Books not italicized include the Bible, the books of the Bible, the Koran, and other scriptures. Titles of poems are not generally italicized, unless they are long poems published under their own right. So we would italicize Spenser's *The Faerie Queene* or Eliot's *The Waste Land*, whereas Yeats's 'The Lake Isle of Innisfree' or Blake's 'The Tiger' are printed in roman type inside inverted commas. Inverted commas and not italics are also used for radio and TV programme titles, short stories, articles and chapter titles.

If you have occasion to print titles in the plural, do not

print the ending in italics. So:

The *Guardian*s were not delivered this morning and we are supplying customers with *Daily Telegraph*s instead.

14.2 Names of ships, aircraft and spacecraft

Normally, these would be italicized. Thus:

the sinking of the *Titanic*
HMS *Invincible* and SS *Nimitz*
Lindbergh's *Spirit of St Louis*
the *Soyuz 12* space mission

14.3 Words or letters which are specially referred to

If you wish to make specific reference to individual words, letters or figures in a printed text, you usually italicize these references. Thus:

The words *separate*, *contemporary* and *liaison* are commonly misspelled.
The following letters are not pronounced: the second *b* in *bomb* and initial *g* in *gnaw* and *gnash*.
She is a messy writer; you will have to dot all her *i*'s for her and cross all her *t*'s.

14.4 Foreign words and phrases not assimilated into English

Some words and phrases have not become fully naturalized in English, even although many people know their meaning. These are written in italics. The decision to italicize or not to italicize will depend to some degree on the text and its intended readership. Generally, words and phrases like ipso facto, ad hoc, al fresco, ex officio, sub judice, wagon-lit, passe-partout, pizza, poppadom, chilli con carne, etc would not be italicized, because they have been widely assimilated. But less familiar words and phrases like *ab origine*, *avis au lecteur*, *ultra vires*, *pax vobiscum*, *mirabile dictu* or *sturm und drang* would be italicized, because they retain a greater element of 'foreign-ness' or obscurity.

14.5 Scientific names of genera and species

In botany and zoology, the name of the genus, or of genus

and species, should be in italic. Higher ranking groups (phyla, classes and orders) are in roman. So:

The buttercups and other plants of genus *Ranunculus* are widely distributed.
One of the most beautiful birds of the order Passeriformes is the waxwing (*Bombycilla garrulus*).
A member of the class of Amphibia.

14.6   Titles of legal cases
These are italicized, so:

Scott v *Metropolitan Police Commissioner* 1974 was an interesting copyright infringement case.
The *Gobitis* case (*Minersville School District* v *Gobitis*) and the *Barnette* case (*West Virginia State Board of Education* v *Barnette*) argued the rights of the American states to require school children to salute the US flag even though that ceremony violates their religious beliefs.

15

Punctuating and Setting Out a Letter

There are one or two points worth noting separately here. They mostly concern the way you lay out your letter (and its accompanying envelope), but they also indicate the punctuation required.

15.1 The envelope and the address

Firstly, addresses normally require no commas nowadays. Thus neither the address of the person to whom you are writing nor your own letterhead needs punctuation marks. Lay out an address as follows:

Mr John Smith MP QC   Mrs Alice Kemble
House of Commons   159 Marine Parade
London SW1   Brighton
          BN2 6QT

A well-addressed envelope has the address towards the left-hand side of the envelope face, so that the postmark does not interfere with it. And it is better if the address is straight and square, not sloping. A is better than B.

A   *B*
Miss C Mitchell OBE   Miss C Mitchell OBE
49 Bentinck Drive   49 Bentinck Drive
London   London
NW5 3PS   NW5 3PS

Remember to avoid introducing unnecessary commas and full stops into addresses, either at the ends of lines or after street numbers.

15.2 The letterhead

The letterhead carries your own address, and the date, at the top right-hand side of the page. Sometimes, at the top left-hand side is also appended your telephone number. Like the envelope, these require no punctuation nowadays, just a clear lay-out. The following is an example:

Tel 0202 664–1257

Flat 2
23 Bulmer Gardens
Bournemouth
Hampshire
BN1 5ZX
16 August 1992

15.3 The letter opening, or salutation

This has two components if it is a formal or business letter, only one if it is a personal letter. In a formal letter, the addressee's name is usually repeated. This is because the letter you have written may be opened by a secretary or an assistant, and the envelope thrown away.

The other opening component of any letter is the salutation, nearly always as follows:

Dear Mr Smith   Dear Mrs Kemble

Note that no punctuation is required here.

The main body of the letter now follows, normally paragraphed and punctuated. The following examples show you how your letters should look. The first is formal, the second is informal:

22 Sevenoaks Road
Dunton Green
Kent
TN13 4ZX
7 July 1992

The Manager
Bristol Hotel
Walmer
Kent
CT14 7BM

Dear Sir
    I am writing ...

15.4   Closing a letter

The letter-ending – or complimentary close – depends on the letter opening. If it is a formal letter addressed to an unnamed person (*Dear Sir/Madam*), the ending has to be *Yours faithfully*. If it is a formal letter but addresses a person by name (*Dear Miss Turner, Dear Dr Bell*), the ending has to be *Yours sincerely*. Informal letters can end in a variety of ways, depending on how well you know the addressee; *Yours, Yours ever, With love*, etc.

This ending goes on a new line, stands as a new paragraph, and requires no punctuation. It is immediately followed by your signature. In formal letters, you type or legibly write your name in full after your signature. The first example is formal, the second is informal:

I look forward to receiving your comments in due course.

Yours faithfully

D. W. Penfold

D W Penfold

Looking forward to seeing you soon.
Love
    David

Punctuation Check-up

Write three short, formal letters and envelopes, set out as suggested in this chapter. Then write two informal postcards. Compare your versions with those set out on pages 93-95.

(a) *Writer's name and address*: Mr David Watkins, 261 Hallam Tower Road, Sheffield S14 2AR. *Date*: 16 December 1992. *Addressee*: The Director, City Housing Department, City Hall, Sheffield S2 1JR. *Request*: A copy of the town's official guide to send to a foreign businessman.

(b) *Writer's name and address*: Ms Antonia Farranti, Via Lampedusa 54, Biancona, Italy. *Date*: 16 January 1993. *Addressee*: The Director of Studies, Crossley School of English, 21 Thanet Gardens, Folkestone, Kent CT16 5AW. *Request*: A place on their language course for foreign students at Easter.

(c) *Writer's name and address*: Your own. *Date*: Today's. *Addressee*: The Tour Manager, Springtours, Wilhelminalaan 132, Delft, Netherlands. *Request*: Book a week's visit to the bulbfields in bloom.

(d) *Writer's name and address*: Your own. *Date*: Yesterday's: *Addressee*: Your nearest relation. *Message*: A postcard note saying you've arrived safely in Paris and done some sightseeing.

(e) *Writer's name and address*: Carlos Jiminez, Cerro de Monterea 14, Campestre San Luis, Mexico 26E5. *Date*: 26 March 1993. *Addressee*: His sister Maria-Elena Jiminez, The Holly Tree Hotel, 15 Palmeira Gardens, Hove, Sussex, BN5 2BB. *Message*: A note to say he's coming to see her next month.

Set out and punctuate the following letters. The first is formal, the second is personal. Check your versions with page 95.

(f) 1172 great western road glasgow scotland 15 january 1993 the manager hotel de catalunya avenida de europa barcelona spain dear sir i wish to book a family room at your hotel for myself my wife and our two children aged 11 and 14 for the eight nights of 6th to 13th august inclusive please quote us your terms if you can offer us accommodation for this period yours faithfully john wishart

(g) the red house offwell near honiton devon march 11th dear aunt elizabeth how nice to get your letter from london and to have news of the wedding im sure it went off very well and i would have loved to be there im making pretty good progress and the doctor says im well down the road to a full recovery he says that i should get the plaster off my legs in the next week or two it can't be a moment too soon for that to happen as im fed up hobbling about the house but im not complaining for a minute and i know ive been very lucky i hope to be fully recovered by the summer holidays and we are all looking forward to see you here in july love from julie

16

American Punctuation

Sometimes you will read a book or an article and observe that aspects of the punctuation are strangely at odds with the guidelines suggested in this book The explanation may be that you are reading an American text, laid out according to the conventions of American rather than British punctuation. As the previous chapters in this book concentrate on the British conventions, a separate note is required for those where the Americans diverge.

American punctuation in essence is very close to British – mercifully. But it is slightly more rigid, and strives more after uniformity. The main differences between American and British practice are in the following details.

16.1 Commas between clauses
There is an American tendency to prefer some punctuation (usually a comma) between clauses in compound sentences. In **1.2** and **3.5**, we said that for British English commas were optional or even unnecessary where there was continuity of subject, instancing the sentences:

> I was late home on Monday because I couldn't start the car.
> She works in the evenings in order to save some money for her holidays.
> He was a keen sportsman and had won a number of trophies.
> She packed an overnight bag and left by the 10 o'clock train.
> Mary felt unwell and she went off to bed.

In an American text, you would probably see all these

sentences set out with a comma:

I was late home on Monday, because I couldn't start the car.

She works in the evenings, in order to save some money for her holidays.

He was a keen sportsman, and had won a number of trophies.

She packed an overnight bag, and left by the 10 o'clock train.

Mary felt unwell, and she went off to bed.

16.2 Commas in lists

There is an American preference for placing a comma in lists to precede the conjunction at the end of a list of three or more items. Whereas British practice favours *x, y and z*, the American preference is for *x, y, and z*. So these sentences (from **3.1**) would be changed as follows for an American text:

British punctuation
They played football, cricket, tennis and rounders.
France, Italy, Germany and the Benelux countries were the founding members of the European Community.
Nick Faldo, Ian Woosnam, Seve Ballesteros and Steve Richardson were members of the Ryder Cup team.

American punctuation
They played football, cricket, tennis, and rounders.
France, Italy, Germany, and the Benelux countries were the founding members of the European Community.
Nick Faldo, Ian Woosnam, Seve Ballesteros, and Steve Richardson were members of the Ryder Cup team.

16.3 Punctuation with quotation marks

The Americans place commas and full stops (but not other punctuation marks) before quotation marks rather than after them regardless of textual logic. Look at the following examples of this difference:

British punctuation
'The man said "yes", not "no".'
By 'abstract object', Professor Poots means 'neither spatial nor temporal", but Platonic in nature. But first a word to distinguish between the terms 'abstract' and 'abstracted'.

American punctuation
"The man said 'yes,' not 'no.'"
By "abstract object," Professor Poots means "neither spatial nor temporal," but Platonic in nature. But first a word to distinguish between the terms "abstract" and "abstracted."

16.4   Double quotes versus single
The American preference here is the exact opposite of the British, and tends to go for double quotes rather than single (*see* **9.3**). And for quotes within quotes, the Americans go for single quotes within double quotes, whereas the British preference is for double quotes within single quotes. This point is illustrated directly above, in **16.3**.

16.5   Punctuation after abbreviations and in numerals
American usage is to follow abbreviations such as *eg* and *ie* with full stops and a comma. British usage often drops this. Americans also continue to use commas in numbers over 1000. So American texts would write:

Don't use vulgar fractions, e.g., write 12.5 rather than 12½.
Always put commas in numbers over 1000, e.g., 1,100 or 5,600,000.

17

Common Errors

In the introduction to this book, I said that it was not my approach to compile a list of 'Thou shalt not's'. However, there are a few very common errors which it is perhaps well to dispose of in the relative quarantine of a short, separate chapter. This list is set out below.

17.1 Full stops
Don't put more than one full stop. If the last word in a sentence is an abbreviation, you don't need to add a second full stop. For example:

I used to work for Wm. Brown Sons and Co.

Nor, as already stated in **1.4**, need you add an extra stop after omission marks. For example:

It's now or never ... do or die ...

17.2 Question marks
Remember not to use question marks after questions in reported speech. For example:

'Can you please tell me the time?'
but
She asked whether I could tell her the time.

17.3 Commas
Writers often forget to use a comma to make their meaning plain. Good writers must pay close attention to detail – otherwise they lose their readers. Compare the following:

(a) John is a keen student of French culture and music.
(b) John is a keen student of French culture, and music.

In (a) the music is French music, in (b) it is music in general.

  (c) Students must answer questions 1 or 2, and 3.
  (d) Students must answer questions 1, or 2 and 3.

These are two radically different instructions. Students take note!

  (e) The students who attend their classes make good progress.
  (f) The students, who attend their classes, make good progress.

In (e) the writer is referring to *some* of the students, in (f) *all of them* are being referred to.

17.4 Apostrophes
Remember:
1. Never use apostrophes for plurals.
2. Never use apostrophes with possessive pronouns:

his	ours
hers	yours
its	theirs

   The only exception to this rule is *one's*.
3. Don't mix up *its* and *it's* (short for *it is*), or *theirs* and *there's* (short for *there is*).

17.5 Brackets
1. Remember always to use brackets in pairs. If you open a bracket, always remember to close it.
2. Never end a line by opening a bracket nor start a line by closing a bracket. If you open a bracket at the end of a line, there must always be at least one word following on before the text goes over to the next line. Similarly, at least one word must always precede a closing bracket at the start of a new line.

17.6 Capital letters
Do not use capitals in any of the following:
1. Subjects in the school or university curriculum – geography, maths, chemistry, comparative theology, psychiatry, epistemics, applied linguistics, etc. *But*, of

course, you need capitals for languages – English, French, Latin, Sanskrit.

2. The four seasons – spring, summer, autumn, winter.
3. Points of the compass – north, south, east, west – unless they form part of the name of a geographical or political entity, for example South Island (New Zealand), Northern Ireland, *but* the east coast of Scotland, a cold front approaching from the west.

But if you abbreviate compass points, you need capitals, for example north-west England and NW England.

17.7 Hyphens

Always remember to distinguish between parts of speech, as in the following:

Noun phrases – no hyphen

She took a keen interest in the architecture of the twentieth century.

The judge gave him a jail sentence of ten years.

'There is a pupil from the third form who wants to see you, Miss.'

The winner signed a contract for three years with MGM.

Compound adjectives – hyphen

She took a keen interest in twentieth-century architecture.

The judge gave him ten-year jail sentence.

'There is a third-form pupil to see you, Miss.'

The winner signed a three-year contract with MGM.

Clauses – no hyphen

Mrs Briggs is a good teacher; but she takes no nonsense.

I don't care what you think – you can take it or leave it.

Adjective phrases – hyphen

Mrs Briggs is a good, no-nonsense teacher.

He has an unsympathetic, take-it-or-leave-it attitude.

18

A Final Check-up

Here are some extra exercises for you to try your punctuation skills on. Answers are on pages 95-99. If you find you are getting the answers wrong, refer back to the relevant chapter.

18.1 Full stops
Write these passages out in proper sentences. Start each sentence with a capital letter and end it with a full stop.

   (a) my cousin Lucy is at the University of Sussex she is finding she has to work very hard (two sentences)
   (b) mrs Pitman has gone to the garage she'll be back in an hour's time i'll tell her you called (three sentences)
   (c) jackdaws look rather like rooks they are sometimes kept as pets with patience they can be taught to mimic human speech but don't forget that jackdaws are mischievous birds they carry off and hide any small glittering object (five sentences)
   (d) there are three ways to get a job done the best way is to do it yourself then you can pay someone to do it for you the third way is to tell your children not to do it under any circumstances (four sentences)

18.2 Exclamation marks and question marks
These sentences need to be punctuated with full stops, question marks or exclamation marks at the end. Other punctuation may also be needed.

   (a) A fine lot of good that will do us
   (b) I am asking all of you if you will subscribe a pound to the cause

(c) If only this toothache would stop
(d) How often do you make the round trip to London nowadays
(e) I wonder how that trick is done
(f) Tom and Barbara are coming with us, aren't they
(g) Tell me why you asked that question
(h) Get out stay out and don't come back
(i) Question what do you call a budgie that's been run over by a lawn-mower answer shredded tweet

18.3 Commas
These sentences need to be punctuated with commas and full stops.

(a) I will not detain you ladies and gentlemen any longer than necessary
(b) Beethoven one of the world's greatest composers was stone deaf towards the end of his life
(c) Fill all the cracks with plaster rub down with fine sandpaper apply a first coat of size allow to dry before rubbing down again if necessary and then apply the first coat of paint
(d) After what seemed like ages we found an area of flattish ground unloaded our gear from the car and began to erect our tent in pitch darkness
(e) He told me frankly that he had telephoned the police and that he didn't care when I went where I went or how I went so long as I left his premises pretty quickly.
(f) According to tradition a bride should carry or wear something old something new something borrowed something blue
(g) They say the unexpected doesn't always happen but when it does it generally happens when you are least expecting it

18.4 Semicolons
Put punctuation marks as needed in the following phrases. All of them will need semicolons, among others.

(a) Swallows migrate vast distances a thousand-mile journey is nothing to these amazing little birds

(b) Like alligators crocodiles lay eggs snakes also reproduce themselves in this manner

(c) Friends Romans countrymen lend me your ears I come to bury Caesar not to praise him

(d) The sun sets night falls very suddenly and after the great heat of the day the desert quickly becomes cold this causes the rocks to split and crumble

(e) A gossip talks to you about others a bore talks to you about himself a brilliant speaker talks to you about you

(f) The items which were found on the beach consisted of a particularly grubby tattered old shirt you wouldn't be seen dead in a pair of old shoes made out of rope string and bits of old tyres and finally a torn and grease- stained pair of overalls

18.5 Colons

Put punctuation marks as needed in the following passages. Most of them will require colons, among others.

(a) We visited many interesting places during our trip to Paris the Eiffel Tower the Champs Elysees the Louvre the Pantheon and the cemetery at Pere Lachaise

(b) This is captain steadman speaking first i'll give you the good news the flight-time is a world record now the bad news because of fog at frankfurt we are having to divert to amsterdam

(c) There is only one way to win wars make certain they never happen

(d) We had quite a shock when we reached home the house had been burgled

(e) Take care of the pennies the pounds take care of themselves

(f) Richard II said not all the water in the rough-rude sea can wash the balm from an anointed king

18.6 Apostrophes

Here are some newspaper headlines. You have to insert the apostrophes, where necessary.

(a) ALL TODAYS TENNIS RESULTS

- (b) NEW ROUTES FOR LONDONS BUSES
- (c) FIRE DESTROYS NURSES FLATS
- (d) LORRYS BRAKES FAIL ON HILL
- (e) SHIPS CREW ADRIFT IN DINGHIES
- (f) PENSIONS FOR SOLDIERS WIDOWS
- (g) CITY GALLERIES FINANCIAL PROBLEMS
- (h) THREE MONTHS RAIN IN TWO WEEKS
- (i) CABINET MINISTERS AT ST PAULS

Correct these sentences by putting in the apostrophes and any other missing punctuation.

- (j) A smiles the way to start the day thats what id say
- (k) Im sorry but youve got the wrong number theres no mike here
- (l) She was in the 85 hockey team when last i saw her shes changed a bit since then of course
- (m) My cousins hands were badly hurt
- (n) Johns watch is five minutes slower than Andrews
- (o) The ladies cloakroom is on the left opposite the mens
- (p) The childrens books were left at my uncles house
- (q) There were displays of babies clothes in the shop windows

18.7 Capital letters
Put capitals and other punctuation in the following sentences, where needed.

- (a) i bought a copy of the daily mail at edgware road and read it on the underground to kings cross
- (b) mr briggs who is irish teaches french and german at st pauls school in hammersmith
- (c) queen elizabeth the queen mother inspected the guard of honour at st jamess palace before going on to the haymarket theatre to see an afternoon performance of the cocktail party by t s eliot
- (d) julius caesar conquered north africa he conquered gaul he conquered britain but before he could take ireland he ran out of conkers
- (e) dr barbara holland consultant at the royal hospital for sick children in glasgow is seen in our picture

caring for scott stephanie and karen a set of very premature triplets from paisley

(f) this term our english class is studying the poetry of john milton last week we read lycidas and for next week we have to study the poem called on his blindness

18.8 Hyphens

Put hyphens where needed in these sentences, along with any other missing punctuation.

(a) The idea of inter continental air travel would have been considered far fetched three quarters of a century ago.

(b) Telling a hair raising story to a bald headed man is a good example of time wasting.

(c) There are twenty seven people in my french class at the franco british institute.

(d) He had one of those insufferable im better than you and you know it expressions on his silly pompous face.

(e) There was a thirty gallon tank in the attic full of the most evil smelling liquid.

(f) A three ton lorry with a top heavy load bumped into a two door sports car at the crossroads.

(g) They were hiding in a bomb proof shelter in the cellar of that prison like building beside the palace.

Remember that phrases do not need a hyphen until you use them as an adjective. Here are some pairs of sentences with words italicized. Which of these words need the hyphens?

(h) Our reporter John Walsh is *on the spot* with the latest news.
Our reporter John Walsh sends us this *on the spot* report.

(i) It was a *never to be forgotten* cup final.
It was a cup final *never to be forgotten*.

(j) The *first night* audience gave the show a good reception.
On the *first night* the audience was enthusiastic.

(k) This timetable is *out of date*, and not to be trusted.
This is an *out of date* timetable, and not to be trusted.

(l) In July, there was a serious crisis in the *balance of payments*.
Things have settled down since the last *balance of payments* crisis.

(m) He is a person with lots of *common sense*.
He is a good, *common sense* person.

18.9 Quotation marks

Punctuate these sentences with quotation marks and any other correct punctuation.

(a) The young man asked have you seen my chisel yes replied my brother you left it on the kitchen table

(b) Oh no cried the boy i don't believe in that sort of thing any more

(c) I hope said the child to her father that you will tell me the story of the african pirate king well smiled her father i may do that but not until you've finished your homework

(d) I believe he's gone to the police station said the young lady to the inspector in a very quiet voice i'm afraid i shall have to ask you too for a statement said the inspector taking out his notebook

(e) I asked John if he was really angry and he answered not really i'm more annoyed than angry

(f) this said miss johnstone looking out of the window is the most important day of my life

(g) if i see anyone move said elizabeth am i to fire at them

(h) do you know a poem called the raven i asked my mother oh yes i think i do she said it was one of those things we had to learn by heart at school its by edgar allen poe isnt is i havent the faintest i admitted but its a clue in todays telegraph crossword do you remember how it went once upon a midnight dreary while i pondered weak and weary began my mother with a weary pondering look on her face thats it i interrupted her ive got it now thanks

18.10 Parenthesis
Put brackets, dashes, or commas – as you think best – in the following. Remember to use pairs.

(a) Now and then as though dreaming she smiled in her sleep.
(b) I shall need a rucksack a really big one for all that gear.
(c) Roger tells me I hope he is right that admission to the castle is free.
(d) The following day Bank Holiday Monday we all went down to Brighton to see the sea.
(e) It was at the nearby town Saumur that we had planned our rendezvous with John.
(f) The officer searched the drawers all the cupboards were locked and he unearthed some useful clues.
(g) I have reached the conclusion having considered all the evidence thoroughly that this young man is innocent.
(h) Grampian Region area 3360 sq m has a population of 475000 The Statistical Yearbook 1990.
(i) Abou Ben Adhem may his tribe increase awoke one night from a deep dream of peace.
(j) People like peaches and pears grow sweet shortly before they begin to decay.

Key to Check-up Sections

Chapter 1

(a) The crocodile lives in the mudbanks of rivers in India and and Africa. His huge body grows to a length of about ten metres. People sometimes hunt him for his leather skin. He has four short legs and can walk reasonably well. But water is his chosen element. Here he can move really fast.

(b) One night a great storm broke over the city. The thunder rolled and roared. The lightning flashed and the rain fell in torrents. Everyone stayed indoors and hid from the elements. Suddenly there was a positive eruption of noise and flashes of blinding light. The bursts came again and yet again. The huddled masses trembled in their hovels.

(c) You have heard of the famous Niagara Falls. Several men have tried to go over these falls in barrels or small boats. In nearly every case the barrels were smashed to pieces against the rocks and the men in them killed or drowned. The only man who ever succeeded in going over the falls was Captain Webb. Later he was to lose his life trying to swim the rapids just below the falls.

Chapter 2

1	?	7	?	13	?
2	!	8	?	14	!
3	?	9	.	15	!
4	!	10	!	16	.
5	?	11	!		
6	.	12	?		

Chapter 3

(a) The opening ceremony took place in the presence of the German economics minister, the Spanish culture minister, the Mayor of Frankfurt, the President of the German Publishers' Association, and the great and good of the European book trade. Also present was a gaggle of gregarious writers, assorted literary glitterati, and of course the ever-watching, omnipresent remainder merchants.

(b) To make cucumber soup, you need one large cucumber, one onion, two ounces butter, one and a half pints white stock, seasoning, and a quarter pint of thick cream. To cook, you need to toss the vegetables in the hot butter for a few minutes, taking care they do not brown. Add the stock, the piece of cucumber peel, and a little seasoning. Simmer for twenty minutes, then emulsify in a liquidizer or sieve. Cool, then blend in the cream.

(c) As well as Mass on Sundays, and her weekly visits to a wayside dance-hall, Bridie went shopping once every month. Cycling to the town early on a Friday afternoon, she bought things for herself, material for a dress, knitting wool, stockings, a newspaper and paperbacked Wild West novels for her father. She talked in the shops to some of the girls she'd been at school with, girls who had married shop-assistants or shop-keepers, or had become assistants themselves. Most of them had families of their own by now. They had a tired look, most of them, from pregnancies, and their efforts to organize and control their large families.

(d) West of the town centre at 2 De Ruyterlaan is the Natuurmuseum, with a collection of rare birds, insects, reptiles and mammals, minerals, and fossils. Nearby stands the Synagogue, topped by a somewhat oriental copper dome. It dates from 1928. East of here is the Boulevard of the Liberation, from which the Langestraat branches off on the left, leading into a street called De Klomp. On the left-hand side is the Elderinkshuis (1783), the only historic building in the town to survive the Great Fire of 1862.

(e) We invited John and Frances for supper, and Mary happened to drop in too. Afterwards we had a long discussion about whether to have a cup of tea, or coffee with rum in it. In the end, David took us all out for a drink. He ordered a whisky and lemonade, a gin and tonic, two dry martinis with ice, three cokes, a lager and lime, and a brandy and soda. I'm glad I wasn't footing the bill.

Chapter 4

(a) This is my umbrella; that is yours.

(b) She told us the whole story; it seemed to go on and on for hours.

(c) That's not fair; I don't think you know the whole story.

(d) I'm afraid I can't find her; she must have left the office.

(e) The doctor did her morning rounds of the wards; she was accompanied by two nurses, a specialist, and a physiotherapist.

(f) The judge passed sentence; the defendant passed out; the press corps sprinted off to relay the news of the verdict to a waiting world.

(g) The chickens had gone; perhaps the fox had got into the hen-house during the night.

Chapter 5

(a) Work fascinates me: I can sit and look at it for hours.

(b) There is a wonderful panoramic view from the top of the hill:

the Castle, the Old Town, the spires, the monuments and the high-rise buildings are all laid out before you.

(c) We climbed four peaks last week: Lochnagar and Mount Keen on Friday, Ben Avon and Cairngorm on Saturday.

(d) There are all sorts of boats in the harbour: yachts, catamarans, speedboats, dinghies, fishing boats, etc.

(e) That has to be one of the surest signs of oncoming old age: when you first notice how young policemen have become.

(f) He is exactly what everyone says he is: a bore and a fool.

(g) The doctor has told her the worst: her husband is not likely to recover.

(h) The following items were stolen: a purse, a ring, cheque cards and a diary.

Chapter 6

(a) can't you've

(b) It's She's I'm John's

(c) car's It'll

(d) train's I'm he'd

(e) It's babies' What's

(f) Women's men's I'm

(g) day's we'd

(h) firm's they've Queen's

(i) Mark's dad's everyone's

(j) school's vandals' It's

Chapter 7

(a) I'm reading *Murder on the Orient Express*, by Agatha Christie. It has to be returned to the library by the end of September.

(b) The English cricket team will visit Pakistan briefly in December on their way back from Australia.

(c) Will the BBC or ITV cover the Arsenal *v* Crystal Palace game on Saturday?

(d) I'm afraid I'm no expert on French or Spanish literature. You should speak to Professor Healey. He teaches French and his wife is from Argentina, I think.

(e) In our geography classes, they used to tell us that America was the Land of Opportunity, and Britain was the Workshop of the World, and the Nile Delta was the Breadbasket of Egypt.

(f) Admiral Nelson was killed at the Battle of Trafalgar and Sir John Moore fell at Corunna.

(g) The 24 bus goes up Whitehall and Tottenham Court Road to Camden Town, and thence to Belsize Park and Hampstead.

But yesterday there was a diversion because of a TUC procession along Euston Road.

(h) The Gaelic language is still spoken today in parts of Scotland, Ireland, Wales and Brittany, but it has completely died out in Cornwall and on the Isle of Man.

Chapter 8

(a) one-eyed
(b) mouse-to-mouse
(c) hundred-strong search-party thirty-odd
(d) corrosion-resistant anti-magnetic
(e) warm-up scrum-half stand-off mid-run hair-raising full-back's up-and-unders cul-de-sac half-time
(f) made-up off-the-peg back-of-the-envelope make-up ice-cream out-patients
(g) mother-in-law Mary-Rose Fotherington-Thomas Henley-on-Thames long-standing dyed-in-the-wool anti-drugs able-bodied eighty-seven-year-old little-frequented
(h) vice-chancellor ex-president non-executive fund-raising two-thirds

Chapter 9

(a) 'Is this the road to the seashore?' asked the motorist.
(b) 'I'm not sure,' replied the young lady. 'I'm a stranger here myself.'
(c) 'I told you to bring a map,' said his wife, 'and now it's too late and all the shops are shut.'
(d) My favourite reading this year has been 'The Ice-Cream War', a novel by William Boyd, and Muriel Gray's funny account of her hill-walking experiences, which is called 'The First Fifty'.
(e) 'I am honoured to receive this award,' announced the MP, 'and I will always cherish it. Thank you very much, ladies and gentlemen.'
(f) 'In the end,' she said, 'we took the umbrella to the lost property office. It was too good an item to simply leave lying in the street,' she added, by way of explanation.
(g) 'The chances of a serious accident,' began the professor, 'are greater than ever. I suppose,' he went on, 'none of you ever considered the possibility of a nuclear explosion, or did you?'
(h) 'But this,' said Angela, 'is murder. I must phone the police,' she added, her voice growing more shrill.

Chapter 10
Passage 1 (A Cool Million)

'I wonder who did it?' asked Steve.

'I can't imagine,' answered Lem brokenly.

'Did they get much?'

'All I had in the world ... A little less than thirty dollars.'

'Some smart leather must have gotten it.'

'Leather?' queried our hero, not understanding the argot of the underworld with which the train boy was familiar.

'Yes, leather – pickpocket. Did anybody talk to you on the train?'

'Only Mr Wellington Mape, a rich young man. He is kin to the Mayor of New York.'

'Who told you that?'

'He did himself.'

'How was he dressed?' asked Steve, whose suspicions were aroused.

Passage 2 (*New Grub Street*)

At eight o'clock came the doctor. He would only allow a word or two to be uttered, and his visit was brief. Reardon was chiefly anxious to have news of the child, but for this he would have to wait.

At ten Amy entered the bedroom. Reardon could not raise himself, but he stretched out his hand and took hers, and gazed eagerly at her. She must have been weeping, he felt sure of that, and there was an expression on her face such as he had never seen there.

'How is Willie?'

'Better, dear, much better.'

He still searched her face.

'Ought you to leave him?'

'Hush! You mustn't speak.'

Tears broke from her eyes, and Reardon had the conviction that the child was dead.

'The truth, Amy!'

She threw herself on her knees by the bedside, and pressed her wet cheek against his hand.

'I am come to nurse you, dear husband,' she said a moment after, standing up again and kissing his forehead. 'I have only you now.'

Chapter 11

(a) Edward (his best friend) ignored Roger in the street.

(b) Eileen Crawford (a woman I have always admired) is coming to our party tomorrow.

(c) We were (still are) happy to see her settled down in a regular job.

(d) No-one in our house (according to my young sister) knows how to dress smartly.

(e) The Royal Family (pictured left) sailed for Norway in Britannia (picture on page 3) this afternoon.

(f) He has a wonderful collection of wild flowers (anemones, primroses and orchids).

(g) Precious metals (gold, silver, platinum, etc) are best kept locked away in a bank vault.

(h) Edinburgh (population 450000) is twice as big as Aberdeen (population 220000) and half as big as Dublin (population 900000).

(i) We spent 45 francs (about £2 sterling) on a trip to some amazing underground caves.

(j) He was a complete eccentric (ate snails, it was said) and his every move was closely watched by all his neighbours.

Chapter 12

(a) Walk, if you please – don't run.

(b) Janice rushed in – and rushed out again.

(c) Cars – those without permits – are only allowed to park for 20 minutes.

(d) I like a good argument – a quiet life is so dull.

(e) No-one believes a word he says – absolutely no-one at all.

(f) Here's a letter from Nancy – what an amazing person she is.

(g) Time we had some decent weather for a change – it's been awful this past fortnight.

(h) My great-grandfather – on my mother's side, of course – was said to have been kidnapped by pirates at sea.

(i) Some recent exhibitions have been very successful – the Egyptian artefacts, for example, were visited by half a million people.

(j) It was Saturday afternoon and the streets were empty – it was as if the whole population was glued to its television screens indoors.

Chapter 13

(a) A student must attempt 3 questions in this exam. S/he should not spend more than 30 minutes on any single question, and s/he should ensure that his/her answers avoid digressions ... No student will be deemed to have passed the exam if s/he scores F on any question.

(b) The individual is described in terms of his/her perception of other members of the group. What is his/her basic position in the group? How far does s/he belong to the group that is influencing him/her? What is his/her overall attitude to the group?

Chapter 15

(a)

261 Hallam Tower Road
Sheffield S14 2AR
16 December 1992

To: The Director
City Housing Department
City Hall
Sheffield S2 1JR

Dear Sir/Madam
Please send me a copy of the official Town Guide to Sheffield for onward transmission to an overseas business contact.
Yours faithfully

David Watkins

David Watkins

(b)

Via Lampedusa 54
Biancona
Italy
16 January 1993

To: The Director of Studies
Crossley School of English
21 Thanet Gardens
Folkestone
Kent CT16 5AW

Dear Sir/Madam
I would like to secure a place on your Easter Holiday English language course. If places are still available, please send me an application form and notify me of the duration and cost of the course.
Yours faithfully

Antonia Farranti

(Ms) Antonia Farranti

(c)

Your address
Today's date

To: Tour Manager
    Springtours
    Wilhelminalaan 132
    Delft
    The Netherlands

Dear Sir/Madam
   I would like to book a week's tour of the Dutch bulbfields during
their flowering season. If you are not completely booked up, please
send me details of itineraries, dates and costs.
   Looking forward to hearing from you.
   Yours faithfully

   Your name

(d)

Paris
Yesterday's date

Dear Uncle Fred,
   Just a short note to say that I arrived safely in
Paris for a few days' sightseeing. Yesterday I
saw Notre Dame and walked along the quays by
the river Seine – very pretty. Tomorrow we are
going to take a train to Versailles. Hope you are
well.
   Love, [Your name]

(e)

Mexico
26 March 1993

Dear Maria-Elena
   This is just a brief word to say that
I'm coming to England next month. I
expect to be there between 11 and 25
April. I hope it will be convenient for
me to visit you and perhaps to stay
with you for a few days.
   Love, Carlos

Maria-Elena Jiminez
The Holly Tree Hotel
15 Palmeira Gdns.
Hove, Sussex
BN5 2BB
England

(f)

1172 Great Western Road
Glasgow, Scotland
15 January 1993

To: The Manager
Hotel de Catalunya
Avenida de Europa
Barcelona, Spain

Dear Sir

I wish to book a family room at your hotel for myself, my wife, and our two children aged 11 and 14, for the eight nights of 6th to 13th August inclusive. Please quote us your terms, if you can offer us accommodation for this period.

Yours faithfully

John Wishart

John Wishart

(g)

The Red House
Offwell
Nr Honiton, Devon
March 11th

Dear Aunt Elizabeth

How nice to get your letter from London and to have news of the wedding. I'm sure it went off very well, and I would have loved to be there. I'm making pretty good progress, and the doctor says I'm well down the road to a full recovery. He says that I should get the plaster off my legs in the next week or two. It can't be a moment too soon for that to happen, as I'm fed up hobbling about the house. But I'm not complaining for a minute, and I know I've been very lucky. I hope to be fully recovered by the summer holidays, and we are all looking forward to see you here in July.

Love from Julie

Chapter 18
18.1

(a) My cousin Lucy is at the University of Sussex. She is finding she has to work very hard.
(b) Mrs Pitman has gone to the garage. She'll be back in an hour's time. I'll tell her you called.
(c) Jackdaws look rather like rooks. They are sometimes kept as

pets. With patience they can be taught to mimic human speech. But don't forget that jackdaws are mischievous birds. They carry off and hide any small, glittering object.

(d) There are three ways to get a job done. The best way is to do it yourself. Then you can pay someone to do it for you. The third way is to tell your children not to do it under any circumstances.

18.2

(a) A fine lot of good that will do us!

(b) I am asking all of you if you will subscribe a pound to the cause.

(c) If only this toothache would stop!

(d) How often do you make the round trip to London nowadays?

(e) I wonder how that trick is done.

(f) Tom and Barbara are coming with us, aren't they?

(g) Tell me why you asked that question.

(h) Get out, stay out, and don't come back! (Or: Get out! Stay Out! And don't come back!)

(i) Question: What do you call a budgie that's been run over by a lawn-mower? Answer: Shredded tweet!

18.3

(a) I will not detain you, ladies and gentlemen, any longer than necessary.

(b) Beethoven, one of the world's greatest composers, was stone deaf towards the end of his life.

(c) Fill all the cracks with plaster, rub down with fine sandpaper, apply a first coat of size, allow to dry before rubbing down again if necessary, and then apply the first coat of paint.

(d) After what seemed like ages, we found an area of flattish ground, unloaded our gear from the car, and began to erect our tent in pitch darkness.

(e) He told me frankly that he had telephoned the police, and that he didn't care when I went, where I went, or how I went, so long asI left his premises pretty quickly.

(f) According to tradition, a bride should carry or wear something old, something new, something borrowed, something blue.

(g) They say the unexpected doesn't always happen, but when it does, it generally happens when you are least expecting it.

18.4

(a) Swallows migrate vast distances; a thousand-mile journey is nothing to these amazing little birds.

(b) Like alligators, crocodiles lay eggs; snakes also reproduce themselves in this manner.

(c) 'Friends, Romans, countrymen, lend me your ears; I come to bury Caesar, not to praise him.'

(d) The sun sets; night falls very suddenly; and after the great heat of the day, the desert quickly becomes cold. This causes the rocks to split and crumble.

(e) A gossip talks to you about others; a bore talks to you about himself; a brilliant speaker talks to you about you.

(f) The items which were found on the beach consisted of a particularly grubby, tattered old shirt you wouldn't be seen dead in; a pair of old shoes made out of rope, string, and bits of old tyres; and finally, a torn and grease-stained pair of overalls.

18.5

(a) We visited many interesting places during our trip to Paris: the Eiffel Tower, the Champs Elysees, the Louvre, the Pantheon, and the cemetery at Pere Lachaise.

(b) 'This is Captain Steadman speaking. First I'll give you the good news: the flight-time is a world record. Now the bad news: because of fog at Frankfurt, we are having to divert to Amsterdam.'

(c) There is only one way to win wars: make certain they never happen.

(d) We had quite a shock when we reached home: the house had been burgled.

(e) Take care of the pennies: the pounds take care of themselves.

(f) Richard II said: 'Not all the water in the rough-rude sea can wash the balm from an anointed king'.

18.6

(a) ALL TODAY'S TENNIS RESULTS

(b) NEW ROUTES FOR LONDON'S BUSES

(c) FIRE DESTROYS NURSES' FLATS

(d) LORRY'S BRAKES FAIL ON HILL

(e) SHIP'S CREW ADRIFT IN DINGHIES

(f) PENSIONS FOR SOLDIERS' WIDOWS

(g) CITY GALLERIES' FINANCIAL PROBLEMS

(h) THREE MONTHS' RAIN IN TWO WEEKS

(i) CABINET MINISTERS AT ST PAUL'S

(j) A smile's the way to start the day: that's what I'd say.

(k) I'm sorry, but you've got the wrong number. There's no Mike here.

(l) She was in the '85 hockey team when last I saw her. She's changed a bit since then, of course.

(m) My cousin's hands were badly hurt.

(n) John's watch is five minutes slower than Andrew's.

(o) The ladies' cloakroom is on the left, opposite the men's.

(p) The children's books were left at my uncle's house.

(q) There were displays of babies' clothes in the shop windows.

18.7

(a) I bought a copy of the *Daily Mail* at Edgware Road and read it on the underground to King's Cross.

(b) Mr Briggs, who is Irish, teaches French and German at St Paul's School in Hammersmith.

(c) Queen Elizabeth the Queen Mother inspected the guard of honour at St James's Palace, before going on to the Haymarket Theatre to see an afternoon performance of *The Cocktail Party*, by T S Eliot.

(d) Julius Caesar conquered North Africa; he conquered Gaul; he conquered Britain; but before he could take Ireland, he ran out of conkers.

(e) Dr Barbara Holland, consultant at the Royal Hospital for Sick Children in Glasgow, is seen in our picture caring for Scott, Stephanie and Karen, a set of very premature triplets from Paisley.

(f) This term our English class is studying the poetry of John Milton. Last week we read 'Lycidas' and for next week we have to study the poem called 'On His Blindness'.

18.8

(a) The idea of inter-continental air travel would have been considered far-fetched three-quarters of a century ago.

(b) Telling a hair-raising story to a bald-headed man is a good example of time-wasting.

(c) There are twenty-seven people in my French class at the Franco-British Institute.

(d) He had one of those insufferable I'm-better-than-you-and-you-know-it expressions on his silly, pompous face.

(e) There was a thirty-gallon tank in the attic full of the most evil-smelling liquid.

(f) A three-ton lorry with a top-heavy load bumped into a two-door sports car at the crossroads.

(g) They were hiding in a bomb-proof shelter in the cellar of that prison-like building beside the palace.

(h) second version

(i) first version

(j) first version

(k) second version

(l) second version

(m) second version

18.9

(a) The young man asked, 'Have you seen my chisel?'
    'Yes', replied my brother. 'You left it on the kitchen table.'

(b) 'Oh no!' cried the boy. 'I don't believe in that sort of thing any more.'

(c) 'I hope,' said the child to her father, 'that you will tell me the story of the African pirate king.'
'Well,' smiled her father, 'I may do that – but not until you've finished your homework.'

(d) 'I believe he's gone to the police station,' said the young lady to the inspector, in a very quiet voice.
'I'm afraid I shall have to ask you too for a statement,' said the inspector, taking out his notebook.

(e) I asked John if he was really angry, and he answered, 'Not really, I'm more annoyed than angry.'

(f) 'This,' said Miss Johnstone looking out of the window, 'is the most important day of my life.'

(g) 'If I see anyone move,' said Elizabeth, 'am I to fire at them?'

(h) 'Do you know a poem called "The Raven"?' I asked my mother. 'Oh yes, I think I do,' she said. 'It was one of those things we had to learn by heart at school. It's by Edgar Allan Poe, isn't it?'
'I haven't the faintest,' I admitted, 'but it's a clue in today's *Telegraph* crossword. Do you remember how it went?'
'"Once upon a midnight dreary, while I pondered, weak and weary ..."' began my mother, with a weary, pondering look on her face.
'That's it!' I interrupted her. 'I've got it now. Thanks.'

18.10

(a) Now and then, as though dreaming, she smiled in her sleep.

(b) I shall need a rucksack – a really big one – for all that gear.

(c) Roger tells me – I hope he is right – that admission to the castle is free.

(d) The following day (Bank Holiday Monday), we all went down to Brighton to see the sea.

(e) It was at the nearby town (Saumur) that we had planned our rendezvous with John.

(f) The officer searched the drawers – all the cupboards were locked – and he unearthed some useful clues.

(g) I have reached the conclusion, having considered all the evidence thoroughly, that this young man is innocent.

(h) Grampian Region (area 3360 sq m) has a population of 475,000 (*The Statistical Yearbook 1990*).

(i) Abou Ben Adhem (may his tribe increase!) awoke one night from a deep dream of peace.

(j) People, like peaches and pears, grow sweet shortly before they begin to decay.

Index

Numbers in **bold type** denote a main section dealing with that item.